Scotland's Pictures

SPONSORED BY BP IN SCOTLAND

SCOTLAND'S
· The National Collection of Scottish Art ·
PICTURES

National Galleries of Scotland

1990

PUBLISHED BY
THE TRUSTEES OF THE
NATIONAL GALLERIES OF SCOTLAND
©
1990

ISBN 0 903148 99 4

DESIGNED BY ROBERT DALRYMPLE
PRINTED IN SCOTLAND BY ALNA PRESS
PHOTOGRAPHY BY ANTONIA REEVE

FRONTISPIECE
A HIND'S DAUGHTER
BY SIR JAMES GUTHRIE

COVER
ALASTAIR MACDONNELL OF GLENGARRY
BY SIR HENRY RAEBURN

Contents

Foreword

This publication is particularly special because within its covers are essays, by scholars on the National Galleries of Scotland staff, about what is undoubtedly the finest collection of Scottish paintings in the world. These collections are separated between the three different galleries that constitute the National Galleries. Sadly, from severe lack of space, far too many of them are normally in store and without a building dedicated to them the chronological and stylistic development will continue to remain very difficult to follow if not totally incoherent.

Never have the National Galleries combined the strengths of their collections to provide the public with a really good opportunity to assess not just the growth of Scottish art but also a lively juxtaposition of masterpieces. In this publication and the associated exhibition we can indulge also in the pleasures of the byeways of the Scottish tradition. Here mapped out is the birth, youth and maturity of the Scottish School, from the shaky first essays of Jamesone to the consummate facility of Raeburn, the introspective portraits of philosophers by Ramsay to the brilliant observation and studied comment of subject pieces by David Wilkie. A new tradition in the late nineteenth and early twentieth century grows out of a graft of French art, with the astonishingly effulgent Scottish colourists, the Glasgow Boys leading to our own day to the 'vigorous' school which has its roots in German expressionism.

This publication and associated exhibition could not have come together without the active enthusiasm and support of the three Gallery Keepers, Dr Duncan Thomson, Michael Clarke and Richard Calvocoressi. The selection has been the task of Lindsay Errington who is the curator responsible for the Scottish School at the National Gallery and, incidentally, served last year as Slade Professor of Fine Art at Cambridge University lecturing on a wide variety of aspects of Scottish Art. She has worked on the concept indefatigably with the helpful collaboration of Dr Duncan Thomson, Keeper of the Scottish National Portrait Gallery and Patrick Elliott of the Scottish National Gallery of Modern Art.

The production of this book and associated exhibition involved much team work from every department and I should like to say thank you to them all – typists, technicians, conservators, handling squad, photographers, Registrars, Administration and Publications departments, and above all Trustees.

The harsh reality of life is that none of this could have been afforded without the financial support of our sponsors BP. I should like to take this opportunity to thank their Chairman, Sir Robert Horton, and their Director, External Affairs Scotland, Mr Ian Sandison.

Timothy Clifford • Director of the National Galleries of Scotland

Sponsor's Foreword

Business flourishes in a flourishing society. To me, it is inconceivable that BP could be as successful if it cut itself off from the communities in which it operates. Our shareholders, our employees, our customers and suppliers, and the community expect us to do what we can to enhance the quality of life – by helping education and young people, by striving to be an industry leader in environmental standards, and by supporting the arts. Commercial success is dependent upon a sympathetic business climate; and this climate cannot be earned without responsible community affairs and environmental programmes.

For these reasons I am delighted that we can support the National Galleries in their endeavour to highlight their unique collection of Scottish paintings. This book, *Scotland's Pictures*, and the exhibition that accompanies it, draw attention to the riches of our Scottish heritage at a moment when interest in Scottish art is at an all-time peak, as evidenced by the prices these pictures now command. BP is happy to be associated with the National Galleries in this creative project to render their Scottish masterpieces more accessible to the community at large.

R. B. Horton • Chairman of BP

Editor's Note

Each of the three National Galleries of Scotland has, from its inception collected Scottish art, with the National Gallery aiming to build up an historical representation of pre-twentieth century Scottish Art, the Portrait Gallery collecting images of celebrated Scots people, painted from life by their contemporaries, and the Gallery of Modern Art acquiring work by modern and living Scottish painters. The present publication was designed to meet the requirements of a guide to the three separate collections of Scottish painting viewed as a single whole. It is arranged, chronologically, to relate the history of Scottish painting – as far as this can be accurately told by means of the existing collections. The only works included are either paintings belonging to the National Galleries or, in a very few instances, paintings on long loan to us. Where the narrative seems unbalanced or omits major artists, this imbalance or bias probably reflects the actual state of the collection, and is something we are constantly looking out to rectify in our acquisitions.

This book, like the exhibition which first accompanied it, covers painting only, excluding on the one hand drawings or watercolours and, on the other, sculpture. These exclusions, which may seem arbitrary, particularly when applied to twentieth-century art, necessarily and regrettably also exclude certain artists. Space, however, dictated the need for some form of limitation and we would hope that sculpture and drawings might be covered in future publications.

Lindsay Errington

IACOBVS · 6 · D · G · R ·
SCOTORVM ·
ÆTA · 29 ·
1595 ·

I

From the Beginnings
to the Early Nineteenth Century

_____

Duncan Thomson

A history of the development of Scottish painting only becomes possible in the closing decades of the sixteenth century. On the periphery of Europe and not economically advanced, the arts of the wider civilisation of which Scotland was a part, tended to take root haphazardly and late. Fragments of mural decoration from the twelfth-century Glasgow Cathedral have survived, but time and destruction have carried away virtually all of the evidence of the painting of the Middle Ages. Inevitably there must have been a good deal of ecclesiastical painting, most of it lost after the Reformation. The paintings of saints and the Crucifixion on the panelled walls of the church at Foulis Easter – in a crude Germanic style – are a rare survival from the middle of the fifteenth century. Equally rare, but of a far greater degree of sophistication, are the two great votive panels painted in the 1470s in Ghent by Hugo van der Goes for the Church of the Holy Trinity in Edinburgh. Besides the figure of the crucified Christ, the panels contain kneeling portraits of James III of Scotland, his queen, Margaret of Denmark, their son Prince James, and the donor, Sir Edward Bonkil.

A form of Renaissance secular art that seems to have become common during the sixteenth century was the triumphal arch, erected for the ceremonial entry of the monarch. Its message was concerned with the continuity of the royal line and it must have contained portraits real, and imaginary. The entry of the young James VI into Edinburgh in 1579 was notable for the quantity of painted decoration (and tapestries) displayed in the streets – 'payntit histories, and ... the effigeis of noble men and women'.

From this type of painting must have developed the portable portrait, usually on a modest scale, that soon became a common feature of court circles. The skills required attracted Netherlandish artists and from this period until the end of the seventeenth century the history of Scottish painting is replete with names that are not Scottish. The earliest clearly identifiable figure is Arnold Bronckorst, an associate of the English miniaturist Nicholas Hilliard, who came to the court in 1580.

1
Adrian van Son
James VI and I
1595

He was succeeded at court in 1584 by Adrian van Son, who was part of a circle of French and Netherlandish painters, goldsmiths, clockmakers and merchants. It is almost certain that Van Son painted the dry, linear image of the king of 1595. It is a remarkably sharp-eyed portrait, flagrantly revealing the single-mindedness of the man, whose principal aim, come what may, was to inherit Queen Elizabeth's throne – something which he was soon to accomplish.

The departure of the court to London in 1603 represents a watershed in Scottish life, the effects of which would be felt until the next great change in the nation's affairs, the union of the Parliaments in 1707. Although the king's accession to the English throne led to a vast widening of the horizons – social, cultural and economic – of those who followed, it inevitably removed the kind of patronage required for the development of an art like painting. Decorative painters, of course, continued to work in large numbers, bringing light and colour and some sense of a world beyond to rooms that were generally small and dark. Indeed an art of bucolic allegories, emblems, and pure decoration flourished in the early decades of the century, usually on ceilings (in effect, the floor-boards of the room above and the joists that supported them). But the growth of a tradition of sophisticated easel painting, represented by painters like Bronckorst and Van Son, was nipped in the bud.

Nevertheless some demand remained and it is evident that a number of the decorative painters turned their hands towards relatively primitive forms of portraiture. And it is from their circles that the first major figure in Scottish painting, George Jamesone, emerges in the 1620s. An Aberdonian, he trained in Edinburgh with a fellow Aberdonian, John Anderson, whose normal range of work included shutters, public clocks, and heraldic and strap-work decoration (the last two feature in the birth-room of James VI which he decorated in Edinburgh Castle). What Jamesone learned in this context it is difficult to say for the portraits he produced into the 1640s suggest experience of a different sort, knowledge certainly of Anglo-Netherlandish portraiture as practised at the new court in London, and perhaps of painting farther afield.

His 'modern' manner – a fullness of form wrapped in a light that picks out shape and colour in a seemingly casual and natural way – is seen at its most beautiful in the portrait he painted of *Mary Erskine, the Countess Marischal,* in 1626. These qualities distance it from the icon-like linearity of Jacobean painting and link it, in its modest way, with the more advanced, Dutch manner, being introduced into England by painters like Cornelius Johnson and Daniel Mytens. Unlike these painters Jamesone was, of course, a native in his own land, which increases his historical significance, for a truly native tradition was longer in taking root in England. This forcing of a local growth can perhaps be seen as an unexpected, long-term benefit of the departure of the court.

Although a handful of other painters, not always identified by name, were

2

George Jamesone
Mary Erskine, Countess Marischal
1626

3
Adam de Colone
George Seton, 3rd Earl of Winton, with his sons George and Alexander
1625

producing portraits in the first half of the century, Jamesone's role was latterly almost completely dominant. Over-production led to a falling away in quality, but such had been his pre-eminence among the burgess, academic and aristo-cratic circles in which he moved that when he died during the civil turmoil that marked the last decade of Charles I's reign, he had acquired a virtually legendary status.

His subsequent reputation, founded on this status, has, however, obscured the significance of a serious rival, the slightly mysterious figure of Adam de Colone. De Colone was in fact the son of Adrian van Son (but for some reason using his mother's name) and he represents a return to the more typically British

DE COLONE

seventeenth-century tradition of dominance by foreign-trained painters. The rather strict formality of his manner which is reminiscent of Dutch painters like Moreelse and Miereveldt suggests that his training may have been in The Hague. Significantly for the career of Jamesone, he was active only in the years from 1622 to 1628, in which year he either died or disappeared onto the Continent. His patrons (who included James VI and I) were almost exclusively those members of the Scottish nobility who had London connections and he seems to have been active there as well as in Edinburgh. Among these clients was George Seton, 3rd Earl of Winton whom he painted with his young sons in 1625. The structure of the portrait has a complexity and basic skills in draughtsmanship that Jamesone was hardly capable of. The substantiality of pigment is an essential part of the compactness of the interlocked forms and the sonorous colour integral to the social and psychological message. It is a painting of watchful solemnity and deep tenderness and is certainly De Colone's masterpiece.

In the years immediately after Jamesone's death in 1644, and during the following decade of Cromwell's Commonwealth, there appears to have been a quite remarkable dearth of painterly activity in Scotland – a reflection of the instability of the times. Some unnamed portrait painters of a provincial sort appear to have been active in the north-east but it is only after the Restoration that identified painters producing substantial numbers of works (almost exclusively portraits) appear – principally the rather crude (sometimes comic) Netherlandish painter Schunemann and the various members of the Scougal family, David, John and George. David begins the new era with a characterful, if rather glum portrait of *Archibald Campbell, Marquis of Argyll,* probably painted shortly before the sitter's execution in 1661. David Scougal's better portraits have a simplicity, and some even a decorative quality, that suggests a connection with the far more sophisticated work of John Michael Wright. The other two members of the family went on working well into the eighteenth century to increasingly crude formulas that must have satisfied for a time, but were latterly seen as being unacceptably archaic.

Jamesone's reputation had been such that in 1636 he had actually attracted an apprentice from London, the young John Michael Wright. Other factors may have played a part, and Wright was certainly of Scottish origin, but it is an interesting reversal of the time-honoured direction of travel. Wright's horizons were, of course, to become far wider than those of most Scottish artists, even the Italophiles of the eighteenth century, with periods in Rome, France, the Low Countries, London, and, late in life, Ireland. Styling himself 'the King's Painter' on the strength of a great state portrait of Charles II, he worked mainly in London but may well have made return visits to Scotland (and he acquired an unidentified, aristocratic, Scottish wife). Among his early works is the wonderfully fresh portrait of the architect *Sir William Bruce*, painted in 1664. The descriptive

4
John Michael Wright
Lord Mungo Murray

WRIGHT

5
John Michael Wright
Sir William Bruce
1664

gesture of *porte-crayon* and drawing and the frank, compelling glance derive from his Roman experience but are also to some extent an expression of what we know of the openness and simplicity of Wright's own character.

Strangely, despite his breadth of experience and the exploratory realism of so many of his portraits, he retained a hieratic element in his art which is almost Jacobean in feeling. That quintessentially Scottish image of the Highland chieftain, the youthful *Lord Mungo Murray* probably painted in 1683, has near-heraldic features that look back to the beginning of the century, although combined with a light-flooded landscape and a perceptual enjoyment of the vagaries of the costume which is wholly modern.

Wright's portrait appears, in fact to have been painted in Ireland, at the end of his long career. It is unlikely to have been seen in Scotland for a number of years, yet it seems echoed in a decidedly native version of Wright's exoticism – Richard Waitt's portrait of *Lord Duffus* painted about 1710. It is an amazingly muscular icon, almost endlessly informational, and a summation of the man's social role. Although Waitt's painting is formally reactionary, he clearly had pretensions to a kind of modernity as his *Self-portrait* of 1728 shows. Naive in drawing, it is nevertheless a cleverly constructed paradigm of the artist's pretensions to status, pointing out – as he does so pointedly – his ability to paint subjects other than portraiture. It is also one of the few erotic paintings in Scottish art.

Records of auctions and inventories, and even surviving work, make it clear that by the beginning of the eighteenth century easel paintings of a wide variety

6
Richard Waitt
Self-portrait
1728

were a common part of the civilised life. Waitt painted still lifes of Scottish fecundity and many houses contained the dead game pictures of William Gouw Ferguson, an expatriate Scot who is more properly part of Dutch art. The one surviving work of Thomas Warrender, who was primarily a decorative painter, is a complex emblem in still life form of the union of the Parliaments of Scotland and England in 1707 and of the dangers posed by Roman Catholicism. But beyond the message is a more internalized assertion: that the cleverness of illusion involved in the painting of a stuffed letter-rack that might be mistaken for the real thing, is a worthy end in itself.

This wider view had already been expressed in a growing dissatisfaction with the forms of portraiture available, and a growing desire among the nobility for what they perceived as the more fashionable London styles. This led in 1691 to the invitation from David, Earl of Leven, to the London-based Flemish painter, John de Medina, to come north. Medina was a contemporary of Kneller and their direct and vigorously brushed manners have much in common. He had not intended to settle permanently but such was the amount of work available that he remained in Scotland after 1693, dying there in 1710. At his best, as in the sensitive study of the aged *Earl of Melville* (father of his principal patron), he is little short of Kneller in accomplishment.

Working in a similar idiom, and initially trained by Medina, was William Aikman who came from the class of the minor lairds – a reflection (as Medina's knighthood in 1707 had been) of a changing perception of the place that the art

7
Richard Waitt
Kenneth Sutherland, 3rd Lord Duffus

AIKMAN

8
Thomas Warrender
Still Life

of painting might take in society. Lacking perhaps the panache of Medina, his work has a sobriety that fits the Augustan age (much of his later career was spent in London where he moved in the circle of Alexander Pope). His *Self-portrait* of about 1715 has a fragile delicacy of light and colour that he rarely equalled, while a late portrait of his friend, the poet *Allan Ramsay*, has an encompassing vigour that is unusual in his work.

The union of the Parliaments had certainly contributed to the prosperity of Scotland and Aikman was one of the earliest of a whole generation of Scottish painters who were now able to familiarise themselves with European art at its source, generally in Italy. John Alexander and his son Cosmo spent prolonged periods in Rome (they had been involved in both Jacobite uprisings of 1715 and 1745 so there were political as well as artistic reasons for their travel); Gavin Hamilton, from Lanark, was to spend virtually the whole of the second half of the eighteenth century in Rome where he played an important role in the neo-classical revival; David Allan spent more than ten years in Italy, studying under Hamilton; Alexander Runciman studied in Rome after an apprenticeship with the decorative painter James Norie and his brother John was to die in Naples in 1768; Allan Ramsay spent formative periods in Rome and Naples; and finally Raeburn, in a sense bringing the tradition to an end, paid a single visit to Rome in 1784-6 – but with little apparent effect on his painting.

Scotland was also now able to benefit from the prosperity of the colonies. A number of painters, perhaps including Waitt, went out to America. John Smibert, who had been born in Gorebridge, after periods of training in London and Italy and a sojourn in Edinburgh, set off for the Americas in 1729, eventually settling in Boston for the final two decades of his life and becoming the virtual

9
William Aikman
Self-portrait

10
James Norie
Classical Landscape with Architecture
1736

founding father of American painting. His portrait of *Colonel Douglas,* painted two years before his departure, shows a hard-fought-for realism – he was never a very natural painter – that was far more accomplished than anything available in America at the time. He was also capable of rather stiff family groups.

Scottish painters also worked in India: George Willison, perhaps best known for his portrait of the young James Boswell (painted in Italy in 1765) spent almost a decade there; the pastellist Catherine Read worked there at the end of her life; and John Thomas Seton painted both Indians and the British there from 1776 to 1785.

THE WARRENDERS & THE NORIES

The new prosperity also meant much greater elegance in architecture and furnishings (for those classes who could afford such things) and, inevitably, greater sophistication in the type of interior decoration demanded. The Warrenders and the Nories, in addition to general house-painting, were now painting canvases for insertion in mouldings above fireplaces and doorways and elsewhere in spacious rooms. The landscapes of the Norie family are generally of a rather watery classicism with notes of strong colour confined to the few small figures who rather aimlessly inhabit them, long vistas on one side and clumps of trees or ruined Roman architecture on the other.

ALEXANDER

These elongated views of a past purely of the mind are unassertive because they were part of a greater whole. The ceiling which John Alexander designed for the Duke of Gordon's great staircase at Gordon Castle in 1720 was rather different. This 'large History picture' which measured some 22 × 20 feet has since vanished but something of its appearance can be guessed from the artist's carefully prepared study (on a scale of 1 : 8.5). The subject is the *Abduction of Proserpine by Pluto* and it is closely based on a design by Giuseppe Chiari with whom

11
John Alexander
Rape of Proserpine
1720

Alexander seems to have trained. Blue sky, finely graduated with an Italian sense of distance, black horses with sharp nostrils, the flaming mouth of Hell where the three-headed Cerberus snarls, the clasped deities, are all intensely particularised. In the four spandrels beyond the framed narrative are grisaille depictions of the spirit and fruit of the four seasons (Pluto was the god of the earth's wealth), sharp in detail – and also in wit: for winter an old man warms his hands above a basin while a bare-footed child ties on skates! Such richness of vision in the large-scale painting (which was also on canvas) must have had a literally brilliant effect in the northern house.

Among the other forms increasingly in demand throughout the eighteenth century were the family group-portrait and its social variant, the conversation-piece. Jeremiah Davidson, although using many baroque conventions, introduced liveliness and naturalness far beyond anything that Smibert had been capable of. Later in the century David Allan takes his families out into the parks surrounding the great houses where parents can admire their capering children – cheerful and rather naive idylls. Allan is particularly associated with the Scottish conversation-piece, a few figures linked in social intercourse in which the painter (or the viewer) takes part more explicitly than in conventional portraiture. This narrative aspect has misleadingly linked his name with that of Hogarth. In fact, far closer to Hogarth in sense and manner (and in time), is the scarcely known Scottish painter, Gawen Hamilton, who painted *Nicol Graham of Gartmore and Two Friends, Seated in a Library*, in the late 1730s. The atmosphere

HAMILTON

12 Gawen Hamilton
Nicol Graham of Gartmore and Two Friends, Seated in a Library
13 John Thomas Seton
William Fullerton of Carstairs and Ninian Lowis 1773

is still and contemplative (although the brush marks are lively), and the passing of time is suggested, no doubt unconsciously, by the curiously detailed painting of the brass lock on the half-open door.

Much of the same stillness, ease and self composure permeates Seton's portrait of *William Fullerton and Captain Lewis*, painted in 1773, some three years before his protracted visit to India. Seton had trained in London under Francis Hayman, whose speciality of small scale full-length portraits had influenced Gainsborough. Seton's figures have a similar compact density, every detail of face, costume and the room bound together in a profound sonority of tone and colour that intimates the relationship between the two men. SETON

These 'portraits' of social situations are in a sense carried into artists' portraits of themselves during the eighteenth century. They are not so much concerned with advertising their increasing status, as they had been in the previous century, as with speaking of their social experience, or of asserting their role within the mainstream of European art and of showing the individuality of their response to the world beyond themselves.

John Runciman painted himself against the cloud-flecked, idyllic blue sky of the Roman Campagna in 1767. But he questions his own existence, and Michelangelo's *Day* from the Medici tomb is disturbed by a violence that speaks of more than the artist's knowledge of a Renaissance memorial. He was to die in Naples the following year, perhaps by his own hand. THE RUNCIMANS

His brother Alexander's *Self-portrait* with fellow artist John Brown is

14
John Runciman
Self-portrait
1767

15
Alexander Runciman
Self-portrait with John Brown
1784

tempestuous in a more direct way. The friends passionately dispute the painter's rendering of a scene from Shakespeare's *The Tempest* and the viewer, who stands where the easel must stand, is drawn into the mysteries of imagination and picture-making.

ALLAN   No such romantic turbulence disturbs the neo-classical calm of David Allan's *Self-portrait*, painted in 1770 for Lady Cathcart who had facilitated his long stay in Italy. He regards himself with ease, even a little narcissism, a chalk drawing by Annibale Caracci lying casually on his table. In a way it is a portrait of having arrived at a destined place – and in terms of colour and design Allan never equalled it.

The self-portraits of Allan Ramsay, both in youth and maturity, suggest that he shared the toughness of character of his father, the like-named poet (whose attempts to establish a regular theatre in Edinburgh had been squashed by the

presbyterian establishment) but his greatest virtues as a painter were to be reticence and delicacy.

After some cursory training in Edinburgh he worked during 1734 in the studio of Hans Hysing in London where he probably acquired some of the toughness of the Kneller tradition. Contact with the empirical vigour of Hogarth must also have been an influence. From 1736 to 1738 Ramsay was in Italy, where he studied with Imperiali in Rome and with Solimena in Naples. He also drew from life at the French Academy in Rome and, uniquely among British portraitists, preparatory drawings were to be a regular feature of his method.

On his return from Italy he set up a studio in London, although he maintained contacts with Scotland. During the 1740s he became immensely successful but his work was very uneven. His hand is scarcely discernible in some signed portraits and at this time he made considerable use of assistants. Nevertheless, there are many portraits where imagination forges a new substance which is a unique compound of sympathy for the reality of being and the materiality of clothes. Among them are the deceptively simple portraits of his first wife, *Anne Bayne*, painted about 1743 – a porcelain smooth face and the upright stalk of her young body endlessly articulated in layers of light – and the elderly *Sir Peter Halkett Wedderburn*, in terracotta coat and every crevice of the marks of time on his face traced with profound feeling.

In the early 1750s Ramsay's style became softer and he edged away from baroque conventions to a rococo lightness that links his work with the French portraitists Aved and Nattier and the pastellists Perroneau and La Tour, the latter of whom he particularly admired. This change is already foreseen in his unsurpassed portrait of the judge, *Lord Drummore,* painted in Edinburgh in the summer of 1754. Nowhere is Ramsay more the painter of the Enlightenment, the portrait a measured interplay between space and tone and the man's rational confrontation with the world beyond his room. The painting coincides with Ramsay's foundation of a philosophical group, the Select Society, whose members included his friends David Hume and Adam Smith, the architect James Adam, the historian William Robertson and Lord Drummore himself.

Shortly afterwards Ramsay set off once more for Rome with his second wife, Margaret Lindsay. His absence until the summer of 1757 had the effect of allowing Reynolds to take over his leading role in London, but that seems to have little concerned him. Having been introduced to the Prince of Wales by Lord Bute, he quickly acquired royal patronage and in 1760, when the prince became George III, he became, in effect, painter to the king.

His French manner reached its apogee in the famous portrait of his wife, painted in the early 1760s. Although it is on a standard size head and shoulders canvas, there is a surprising sense of lateral movement, the figure turning from the domestic reality of the window shutter on the left (with daylight entering

18
Allan Ramsay
Sir Peter Halkett Wedderburn
1746

19
Allan Ramsay
Hew Dalrymple, Lord Drummore
1754

20
Allan Ramsay
The Painter's Wife (Margaret Lindsay)

21
Allan Ramsay
David Hume
1766

only from the upper half of the unseen sash window) towards the confection of roses and vase on the right. The movement of the layers of lace on satin and the barely flushed delicacy of the gentle face give the portrait a breathtaking poignancy.

The portrait of *Mrs Bruce of Arnot,* which he painted a year or two later, takes virtually the same structural form as the portrait of Anne Bayne, painted at least twenty years earlier, but the fragility of the means are entirely new. The pigment of the face is endlessly fragmented into a shimmering luminescence, yet the sharp edge of the woman's personality shines through, both mysterious and straightforward.

Ramsay's painting career had virtually finished by the end of the decade. His royal patronage had brought the ease required to pursue his literacy and archaeological interests and to travel. He was to die at Dover in 1784 as he returned from the last of his visits to his beloved Italy.

22
Allan Ramsay
Mrs Bruce of Arnot

23
Allan Ramsay
Jean-Jacques Rousseau
1766

Among the last of his portraits were two of the greatest figures of this age of Enlightenment, which Ramsay himself had so graced, his old friend *David Hume* and the exiled *Jean-Jacques Rousseau*. Hume tried to care for Rousseau during his stay in England and commissioned both portraits. His own is four-square, as that of Lord Drummore had been, graceful and sympathetic despite the reality of his frog-like appearance, while that of Rousseau lights up the fresh intelligence of the man. But by this time Rousseau moved in an inner darkness of paranoia and he came to believe that Ramsay had set out to show how handsome Hume was compared to his Cyclopean self!

Copies of the portrait had been made by Ramsay's assistant David Martin, and it is not unlikely that it was one of these that Rousseau was referring to, rather than the original. Martin, who worked with Ramsay for a number of years, lacked the latter's subtlety but he had an enquiring mind and an individual strength in his quest for appearances. These are qualities, allied to some of

RAEBURN

Ramsay's grace, that are evident in the portrait of *Professor James Russell and his Son* which Martin painted in 1769, shortly before he took up permanent residence in Edinburgh.

Martin links the exquisite art of Ramsay, which was grounded in the Scottish tradition, with the vigorous art of Henry Raeburn which brought that tradition to a culmination. There is evidence that he helped the young, largely untrained, painter in his earliest years and that Raeburn learned a good deal by copying his portraits. But Raeburn's natural gifts were so phenomenal that he soon went on to forge a style so individual that the age of which he himself became so significant a part is now seen by us largely through his eyes. This virtually defining quality is something that not even Ramsay, perhaps because of his divided loyalties or the wider field in which he moved, had been able to attain.

Raeburn was initially trained by a jeweller, James Gilliland, with whom he discovered an ability to paint miniatures. He then developed, largely by his own efforts and with whatever help he received from Martin, into a painter of life-size portraits. Among the earliest is the seated portrait of the geologist, *James Hutton,* whose research into the life of the earth was leading to his unsettling (even for that enlightened age) conclusion that he saw 'no vestige of a beginning – no prospect of an end'. Owing something to Martin in its arrangement, it may be as early as 1778, when Raeburn was twenty-two. The pose is hardly felicitous and his left shoulder has a strange encounter with the back of the chair, but there is a strong sense of the man's questioning mind and passages such as the hands

26
Sir Henry Raeburn
Lieutenant-Colonel Lyon
1788

and the pile of specimens and books are beautifully observed and painted with
fluidity.

In marrying Anne Leslie, a widow of some means, in 1780, Raeburn achieved
financial security and four years later he took the well-trodden path to Italy. He
made contact with Reynolds in London *en route* and this seems to have affected
the portraits he painted on his return more than his two years abroad. This influence is most evident in the portrait of *Admiral Inglis,* which has a good deal of
Reynolds's high seriousness. The portrait of *Lieutenant-Colonel Lyon* which he
painted about the same time also has something of Reynolds's compositional
drama but the creamy pigment, high key and strong colour may recall something seen in Italy. Whatever it was, it was soon forgotten, for by the early 1790s
his use of pigment had become drier (but no less bold) and he was beginning to

27
Sir Henry Raeburn
The Reverend Robert Walker Skating on Duddingston Loch

explore how strong light could be used to define mass and outline. The expressive possibilities of contour soon led to an interest in the profile of the human face, and he modelled (with a jeweller's ingenuity) his own profile in 1792 which was then cast by the medallionist, James Tassie. At least two of his paintings of the early 1790s continue this interest, one a portrait of *William Glendonwyn* (at Cambridge), the other the famous small full-length of the *Reverend Robert Walker Skating*. The scale is unexpected for Raeburn but the dark figure silhouetted with a perfect precision against sky and ice, the tonal refinement of the profiled face, and the shadow of the hat rim that falls across it are all completely in line with his interests at this time. The same cast shadow occurs in the portrait of *David Hunter of Blackness* which must also date from the early 1790s, the same definition of dark shape against light distance and, despite the difference in scale, the same modulation of the surface of the faces.

28   Sir Henry Raeburn
David Hunter of Blackness

During the later 1790s Raeburn developed the breadth of handling which was to be his hallmark and the sympathy with his sitters which was to make his work so popular. On the strength of his growing success he moved in 1798 into a spacious terraced house in York Place, the painting room of which he adapted to create the strong downward effects of light that he would favour until the end of his career.

He now had few rivals. Martin had died the previous year and the pastel portraits of Archibald Skirving posed no threat. These were sensitive and had a dense brilliance, as the portrait of *Mrs John Wilson* shows, but both his methods of working and his relationship with his sitters were erratic. George Watson, who had trained with Alexander Nasmyth, worked in a stylised version of Raeburn's own manner which could hardly stand comparison. Nasmyth himself (who lived on the opposite side of York Place) had turned to landscape after his radicalism had lost him his portrait practice. His small full-length portrait of the poet *Robert Burns* (which has become a national icon) recalls the portraits in landscapes at which he had once excelled. Based on his cabinet portrait of 1787 it was painted long after the poet's death.

29   Archibald Skirving
Mrs John Wilson

What may have been one of the earliest portraits to come from Raeburn's new studio was the glamorously coloured full-length of *Sir John Sinclair,* probably painted in 1799 on the disbandment of his Rothesay and Caithness Fencibles. Compared to Benjamin West's similar portrait of Sinclair, on which Raeburn appears to have based his design, it is wonderfully relaxed and natural. These are qualities that typify the portraits which he painted over the next ten to twelve years, of a society that he gives a sense of seeming to understand its own history. To this end his hand develops an almost Halsian speed and deftness (he painted direct, with no preparatory drawing) and a fulgent chiaroscuro.

He exhibited regularly at the Royal Academy (and even contemplated moving to London in 1810) and the paintings he sent there tend to have a greater

30   Alexander Nasmyth
Robert Burns

31
Sir Henry Raeburn
Colonel Alastair Macdonell of Glengarry

31A
Detail

than normal degree of finish and contrivance. Among them is the 'monument' of 1812 to the romantic Jacobite, *Macdonell of Glengarry* (who in reality deserved no monument), which it is difficult not to compare with the great Highland chieftains of Wright and Waitt – and Scott was to say of the subject, 'he seems to have lived a century too late'.

This misplaced desire to impress a London audience marks Raeburn's *Self-portrait* of 1815, which he seems to have worried over to distraction, even going to the extent of rotating the canvas on its stretcher to give his body greater up-rightness and presence. Many of his later portraits became increasingly mannered, his women, like *Mrs Scott Moncrieff*, turning long necks and liquid eyes towards some estatic vision, the men contemplating their own apotheosis. This sense of a reputation defined for all time is the key to the portrait Raeburn painted of that other great figure of this golden age, *Sir Walter Scott*, completed shortly before the painter's death in 1823.

Although the painting of the nineteenth century now increasingly turned in

WATSON GORDON   other directions, Raeburn's legacy lived on in the work of Sir John Watson

33
Sir Henry Raeburn
Self-portrait

Gordon – at times mundane and descriptive, but often lively and sympathetic. As late as 1830, in Gordon's portrait of the other peasant poet, *James Hogg*, Raeburn's tradition of sense and sympathy, now invested with Gordon's realism, continues to enliven Scottish painting.

34
Sir John Watson Gordon
James Hogg ('The Ettrick Shepherd')

II
The Nineteenth Century

Lindsay Errington

Reviewed after the passage of almost another complete century, the nineteenth century can now be recognised as a period of tremendous growth and increase in the variety, veracity and imaginative power of painting in all Western nations, especially in the smaller countries. In the late eighteenth century, Scotland possessed a school of design, the Trustees' Academy, publicly funded to turn out commercial designers. It possessed almost no other artistic facilities. Painters did nonetheless emerge from the Trustees' Academy, and also from the workshops of coach painters, or from the private studios of the portraitists of the day, and, if they were lucky, these emergent artists found patronage and commissions for more portraits from landowners and businessmen. The commissioned portrait and the bespoke decorative picture, designed to fit an interior architectural scheme, dominated the production of native art. In a sense what the patron required of the native artist was not art at all – if by this is meant a vehicle for aesthetic and imaginative experience – but a record or embellishment of himself and his property. And it was not in Scotland but in Rome that the eighteenth-century Scottish painter found an outlet for the exercise of a tragic or light-hearted visual imagination.

By the end of the nineteenth century the situation was transformed. There were art schools in the major Scottish cities. There were National Galleries in Edinburgh, and public collections in many of the other large towns. There was the Royal Scottish Academy, and numerous other artists' societies holding regular exhibitions had also sprung up, along with dealers buying and selling modern Scottish art and importing recent works from the continent. There was an enormous increase in the range of possible subject matter, which now comprised landscapes, real or imaginary, and imagined scenes from poetry, legend, history, and daily life.

The work of John Runciman, the short-lived brother of the better known Alexander, painted on a small scale, and only surviving in a very small quantity, anticipates the romanticism of much later Scottish art. The turbulent background of castle, cliff and storm-thrashed sea, in his *Lear*, represents an emotive

36
Gavin Hamilton
Andromache Bewailing the Death of Hector

37
David Allan
The Origin of Painting
1775

35
Alexander Nasmyth
The Building of the Royal Institution
1825 (detail)

38
John Runciman
King Lear
1767

RUNCIMAN approach to Shakespeare's text, as the viewer is invited to re-experience, through visual equivalents, the anguish and fury of the poetry. Unlike the be-spoke painting, which could only be of interest, as an object of possession, to one particular patron, such a work as *Lear* offers itself to the understanding of any imaginative viewer. In Runciman's tiny but impassioned picture we see the promise of a new figurative painting which was to materialize in the ensuing century.

WILKIE It is hard to imagine the subsequent course of Scottish art without Wilkie. If Raeburn's portraits could be removed *en bloc* out of history, we should lose a great deal of fine painting, but if Wilkie's *oeuvre* were similarly excised much subsequent Scottish painting would remain quite puzzling, and the viewer would look about in vain for some common source or explanation. It is equally hard to determine how far Wilkie was a shaper of, or how far he was shaped by his age. Subject painting in Scotland certainly needed a figure of his qualities, just as the miscellaneous mass of ballad, legend and historical matter, both oral and written, which the nation had accumulated, needed a writer like Scott to give it vital form. Works such as *Pitlessie Fair*, *The Penny Wedding* (belonging to Her Majesty the Queen) and the *Knox dispensing the Sacrament at Calder House* (unfinished though both versions of this are), made visible and positive, in a memorable form, the secular folk tradition and the religious history of Wilkie's native land. Both the last two pictures have become, in some sort icons. Both themes, the rural wedding dance, and the career of Knox, had already been tack-led by Wilkie's eighteenth-century predecessor, to whom he owed so much, David Allan.

39 Andrew Geddes
Portrait of David Wilkie 1816

Allan's *Highland Wedding at Blair Atholl* with its lively dancers reeling to the fiddle music of Niel Gow, had been painted after the artist's return from a prolonged stay in Italy, and it seems to have been regarded by Allan as the native Scottish version of the dancing Italian peasants whom he had already drawn in Naples. Such paintings as this were circularised by Allan in the form of watercolour replicas and etched prints. They appealed to a rising local interest in the rural cultural traditions of Scotland as they served to distinguish it from its neighbour. Wilkie drew on the same interest, but, unlike Allan, was able to market his paintings of Scottish folk life much further afield, amongst English collectors, to whom the romance of things Scottish had also now extended.

Wilkie was a phenomenon. To the public of London, on whom he broke overnight, at the R.A. exhibition of 1806, and who did not know his background of art education at the Trustees' Academy of Edinburgh, he was the un-taught rustic prodigy *par excellence*. What were his real qualities? In the first place an ability to absorb and reflect back the character of the then popular seventeenth-century Dutch and Flemish artists, secondly, extreme skill in grouping and arranging figures, and delicacy and sensitivity in painting them, lastly, a most remarkable observation of and appetite for all the nuances of gesture and behaviour by which people indicate their characters, thoughts and feelings. His

40
David Allan
A Highland Wedding at Blair Atholl
1780

41 Sir David Wilkie
*William (Chalmers) Bethune, his Wife
Isobel Morison and their Daughter
Isabella* 1804

42
Sir David Wilkie
Pitlessie Fair
1804

43
Sir David Wilkie
The Letter of Introduction
1813

44
Sir David Wilkie
John Knox Dispensing the Sacrament
at Calder House (study)
*c.*1837–40

LIZARS GEIKIE
& HARVEY

subjects were not, generally at that point, overtly Scottish. That came later, after a definite decision taken by him in 1817 – encouraged perhaps by the success of Scott's *Waverley Novels* – that he would make his subjects more Scottish in future. Shown in Edinburgh exhibitions intermittently from 1821 onwards, Wilkie's key paintings acted as a spur and stimulus to other artists, and also maybe as encouragement, demonstrating just how high the Scottish artist might reach, through innate ability, in the competitive London art world. Wilkie left in Scotland disciples of his style and subject matter, both high – history painters – and low – rustic genre painters. Indeed the little group of early nineteenth century genre painters who owe a debt to Wilkie, from the older Alexander Carse, to Lizars and Walter Geikie, and Sir George Harvey in his earlier work, are one of the charms of Scottish art at this period. They knew their limitations and worked within them. Their little pictures are imaginative, truthful, unsentimental – the best that any local school could produce – and they serve to record,

45
William Home Lizars
Reading the Will
1811

46
Walter Geikie
Scottish Roadside Scene

47
Sir George Harvey
The Curlers (study)
*c.*1835

as was surely intended by their makers, habits of life and work typical of rural Scotland and, even then, passing out of use.

The expanding scope and range of figurative painting in late eighteenth and in early nineteenth-century Scotland was matched by similar developments in landscape painting.

Landscape painting which, in the late nineteenth century, became the vehicle of one of the most expressive and least conformist painters Scotland ever produced – William McTaggart – was also, at the beginning of the century, a direct means of escape for the artist from the constrictions of the formal commission into a world of personal expression and sentiment. Only a landowner could of course possess nature, or would order a portrait of his estate. Any person of taste and sensibility could enjoy nature, and might choose to buy a painting which

48
Jacob More
The Falls of Clyde (Cora Linn)

49
Alexander Nasmyth
The Building of the Royal Institution
1825

expressed that enjoyment in a way he could share. Alexander Nasmyth, un-popular, as a known radical sympathiser, with the powerful Scottish landed families who had supplied him with portrait commissions, evaded their power and control by abandoning portraiture and turning to the ready-made – as op-posed to the bespoke – landscape, which rested its appeal on expression and sen-timent instead of ownership. He was not, of course, entirely the first artist to do so. In the previous century Jacob More's views of the scenic chain of waterfalls on the River Clyde had not, as far as we know, been painted for the proprietors of the sites, but for the sensitised tourist who liked to visit large falls and shudder with awe as the spray flew up into his face. Nasmyth, however, and his numer-ous family – most of them also competent artists in the family style – set a very personal stamp onto Scottish landscape painting, mainly perhaps because of the sheer quantity of work they turned out.

MORE

Nasmyth's landscapes were not popular amongst later critics, who found them, compared with Thomson of Duddingston's paintings, lacking in fervour, and tepid in their expression of the wilder aspects of Scottish scenery. They need to be understood as standing in a direct line of succession that passed from the

NASMYTH

workshop manner of the decorative Norie firm, on to the magnificent panoramas of David Roberts. One factor in this tradition is a high level of technical accomplishment – which at its lowest point can degenerate into sets of systems for foliage, water or skies. This systematic professionalism imposed certain limitations on the individuality of the artist's expression, whilst never allowing his work, even at its least inspired, to drop to an unacceptable level. The ingredients of this landscape tradition are the components of human civilization and social relations – people, architecture and nature in an appropriate balance.

The content of Nasmyth's landscapes directly reflects his own interests in design, town planning, construction and engineering, as well as in nature, natural science and geology. His friends were intellectuals like Hutton the geologist, with whom he used to stroll around Edinburgh, discussing natural phenomena. This scientific bent has much to do with the content of pictures such as *The Building of the Royal Institution*, with its lavish foreground explanations of scaffolding and machinery, as as well as with the reminiscing *Edinburgh Castle and the Nor' Loch*. The latter is both a recollected record of the raw site before its New Town planned alterations, and of the geology of the primitive rock on which the Castle stands.

THOMSON

In the history of Scottish landscape painting the amateur Reverend John Thomson occupies a position of eminence which his ability as a painter by no means qualifies him to hold. Indeed if he is to be assessed simply as a painter, the claims his admirers have made for him – including some admirers who should have known better – and the mounting of his fame on a pinnacle higher even than Turner's, will leave the impartial viewer very puzzled indeed. His subject

50
Alexander Nasmyth
Edinburgh Castle and the Nor' Loch
1824

matter is repetitive, his imagination stereotyped, his colour often muddy or leaden, his draughtsmanship and understanding of form rudimentary and his oil painting technique amongst the most unstable and gimcrack in an age devoted to unstable and experimental techniques. Neverless the work of this devoted amateur still retains the ability to seize and grip the imagination. It is obvious that Thomson did posses some special power, though what that power was, may be less obvious.

Amongst all genres, landscape painting offers the amateur who has never learnt the elementary rules for understanding and reconstructing solid forms on a flat surface the easiest route to disguise his weaknesses. Thomson's ignorance of draughtsmanship may even, perversely, have been an advantage to him. What he offers us is not rocks and stones, castles or mountains, but a display of naked emotion – the landscape of the inside of the human mind projected upon the features of the exterior world. The turbulent but formless unindividualised character of his rocks or seas or disintegrating ruins makes them just sufficiently recognizable for what they are and no more. They are equivalent to symbols or mental concepts of stormy seas and trackless cliffs, not portraits of real ones. His active brushwork, with its loaded impastos, squirls, streaks, loops and blotches, generates a sense of tension and excitement quite independent of its descriptive capacities.

Nevertheless many of Thomson's fantastic landscapes do bear real place names, and in this lies the secret of his Scottish reputation. By turning all these intense and passionate feelings onto identifiable Scottish locations, he validated the very landscape itself, presenting it as the source of profound emotion. His

51
The Rev John Thomson
Fast Castle from Below
possibly 1824

paintings, especially the numerous versions of *Fast Castle*, acted on contemporary viewers as translations into paint of the literary work of Sir Walter Scott – translations, not of Scott's actual words, but of the emotion behind them.

Thomson's nearest counterpart in the world of imaginative figure painting was probably David Scott. The personal, autobiographical quality with which Scott endowed his paintings, is at once their strength and their weakness. By a process of identification the hero of each of his pictures was turned into the artist himself, and the process of self identification enabled Scott's paintings to embody very highly charged personal emotions. The force of emotion as it reaches the viewer in, for example, *The Traitor's Gate*, can be frightening – all the more so as the uneasy viewer begins to discover that the grip being exerted on his own psyche is that of a very disturbed and neurotic personality. 'Squareness', Scott wrote 'is most characteristic of death: roundness of life' and in the square, and toothed black grid of the portcullis that cuts off the circular segment of open sky and life, he exploited an image which appeals to the most basic and elementary human terrors – terror of darkness, claustrophobia, entombment, the menace of the unknown unseen human agents, of blades, bars and spikes all closing in on the central victim. The psychological engineering is that of Mrs Radcliffe's *The Italian* or of later stories by Edgar Allan Poe. Scott's paintings are so much renderings of the interior self that they scarcely qualify as history paintings in the sense that Wilkie or William Allan would have understood the term. It is in this way that they seem the counterparts of Thomson's land or seascapes – direct attempts to find the most immediate sensory equivalents to inward experience, and marred, as Thomson's pictures are marred, by the inadequacy of Scott's

52
David Scott
The Traitor's Gate
1842

53
Sir William Allan
The Murder of David Rizzio
1833

54
Sir William Allan
The Slave Market Constantinople
1838

draughtsmanship and technique.

The already mentioned William Allan, an older and saner history painter than Scott, was a friend of Wilkie, who had studied in Edinburgh at the same classes but who, apart from extensive and prolonged travel in Russia and the Near East, elected to pass his artistic life in Scotland, where he became president of the Royal Scottish Academy in 1837. He was also a friend of Sir Walter Scott, and the influence of both Scott and Wilkie is strong in *The Murder of Rizzio*, with its vividly imagined rendering of violence and terror, its flaring torches and deep, bituminous shadows. His *Slave Market*, a product of a later visit to Constantinople, anticipates, in its brighter, cleaner colouring, Wilkie's own studies

of oriental character and dress, painted on his last, fatal, Eastern journey, and is a reminder that the kind of romantic orientalism to be found in the French artists, Decamps, Delacroix and Vernet, was not confined to France, and that Scottish artists at this date were far from provincial in their outlook.

The short-lived Thomas Duncan, a talented pupil of William Allan, was another practitioner of the Wilkie/Allan style who did not survive to produce the work of which he might have been capable.

The last important exponent of the Wilkie/William Allan tradition of history painting was Robert Scott Lauder. He is valued sometimes only as a link between the early and later centuries, since he became the teacher of George Paul Chalmers, William McTaggart, John Pettie and William Quiller Orchardson. Nevertheless his work deserves consideration in its own right. Influenced by the use Wilkie and Allan had made of the contrast between opaque and solid highlights with thin, translucent shadows Lauder's taste for 'painterly' handling and for colour, was enhanced by his study of Etty's large pictures at the Royal Scottish Academy and Venetian Art in Italy.

At a date when German-influenced history painting with its severity of outline, stress on correct drawing and somewhat arid colour, had a stranglehold grip on the British efforts to establish a tradition of public mural painting, Lauder made a valiant though unsuccessful attempt to establish a counter-style. His *Christ Teacheth Humility*, his entry for the 1847 Parliamentary Competition held

55
Thomas Duncan
Portrait of 'Christopher North'
(*Professor John Wilson*)

56
Robert Scott Lauder
Christ Teacheth Humility
1847

in Westminster Hall, London, shows what he had learnt from Wilkie – especially perhaps the last, unfinished *Knox* – from the orientalism of William Allan, and, perhaps also from the work of a much more thorough-going orientalist and traveller than Allan, Lauder's own friend David Roberts.

Born in Stockbridge, and carrying his Edinburgh accent and his air of a prosperous Scottish businessman, to the end of his days, most of those days were, nevertheless, spent by David Roberts in travelling abroad and collecting material for his pictures. He could paint on a large scale, putting in huge and complex architectural features and dramatic effects of light with effortless assurance and deftness of touch – skills which he must have owed to his early work on theatrical scenery. He was a product of the painter/decorator and

57
Sir David Wilkie
The Irish Whiskey Still
1840

ROBERTS

58
Robert Scott Lauder
David Roberts in Oriental Dress
1840

theatrical designer tradition which, as already stated, had passed from the Nories down through Alexander Nasmyth – all painters of landscape with architecture. Roberts' panoramic view of Rome (which he presented to the R.S.A. in order that it should be displayed in the National Gallery of Scotland) effectively displays his particular mastery of architecture and unexpected lighting. Skill, knowledge, control and efficiency are as necessary qualities to such virtuoso public displays in the theatrical tradition as they are irrelevant to the tradition of Thomson of Duddingston, in which intense personal experience is privately communicated from artist to viewer.

MCCULLOCH

It is sometimes a little hard to decide which of the two traditions Horatio McCulloch belongs to. His earliest paintings owe a good deal to Thomson, and his preferred subject matter – castles, lochs, wild glens and huge mountain shoulders – also derives from Thomson. It was, however, through the popularity of Sir Walter Scott's poems and novels, just the kind of scenery that was now regarded as quintessentially Scottish by the annual droves of tourists to the Highlands, and along with all McCulloch's undoubted superiority to Thomson in matters of technique and draughtsmanship, there is a quite perceptible debasing or commercialising of the emotional quality in his paintings. His *Inverlochy Castle* is undoubtedly bigger, better drawn and better coloured than most Thomsons. But it is not necessarily a better picture, and it bears an alarming resemblance to a jumbo-sized picture postcard. It was not until William McTaggart had evolved his mature style in the 1880s that the art of conveying a personal response to the natural world with integrity and truth, and on a large scale, was recovered.

McCulloch's work has stylistic features in common with that of the mid-century Scottish figurative painters – a certain hardness, and an attention, even over-attention to detail. These men, James Drummond, William Fettes Douglas and Joseph Noel Paton, were the most erudite of artists. They were members of the Society of Scottish Antiquaries, and were collectors in their own rights, collectors of books, of armour, medals, ceramics, carving and Scottish and other antiquities. This erudition and acquisitiveness spills over into

60
Horatio McCulloch
Inverlochy Castle
1857

61
James Drummond
The Porteous Mob
1855

every cranny of their intensely detailed, over-filled paintings. Drummond's passion for old Edinburgh with its tall, crazy, tottering tenements is as much his motive for painting *The Porteous Mob* or *Mary Queen of Scots* as any desire to reconstruct an episode in Scott's novel *The Heart of Midlothian* or to express the challenge that Mary – martyr or murderess? – has set all subsequent Scottish historians. The subjects that these artists selected must have been far, one supposes, from the normal run of popular taste or general knowledge. Of the three, Fettes Douglas was possibly the most elusive and recondite. His pictures are like extended still lifes in which humans play a minor role, along with books and im-

plements of alchemy and magic. Such stories as they possess are left for the viewer to work out. They do not usually illustrate given texts, and, unlike Drummond and Paton, Douglas had a sense of the value of empty as well as filled space, which he used to good effect in *The Spell*, and which seems to have been transmitted later to Pettie and Orchardson.

Paton's *Quarrel of Oberon and Titania*, companion to his earlier *Reconciliation*, is one of the few major paintings of its day with the academic nude for subject. It is a Bacchanalian revel, presided over by a herm of Pan, in which the idealised nude – both male and female, but mainly female – is presented in every pose and

62
Sir William Fettes Douglas
The Spell
1864

NOEL PATON

from every viewpoint. The life studies alone which this entailed, not to mention the studies of plants, snails, lizards and spiders, must have cost the artist months of work. The finished object is a cornucopia of knowledge of the natural world and of classicising aesthetic theory, all offered in the setting of fantasy. The *Luther at Erfurt*, which catches the Protestant Reformer at the very moment of his dawn revelation of the doctrine of salvation by faith, is typical both of Paton's erudition and of his mania for collecting. Luther, grasping a huge Bible, opened at one of Paul's Epistles, is surrounded by rejected litter of books by accepted Catholic theologians. His crisis of faith, conveyed in his anguished expression and again in the material objects of his surroundings – if they are emblematically, allusively and otherwise correctly 'read' – produced the most truly Pre-Raphaelite picture of Paton's career.

Many Scottish artists of the mid-century, whether, like Noel Paton, Fettes Douglas and James Drummond, they stayed in Edinburgh, or like Dyce, moved to London, or like William Bell Scott, oscillated between the north and south, tend to be marked by the clearness of their outlines and the intricacy of their details. Occasionally, in the work of Paton and Drummond, the passion for detail, precision and finish leaves the viewer with the impression that these pictures, like the furniture, carpets and ironwork of the period, have really been machine-made. Despite closest scrutiny, the surfaces resist the spectator's efforts to find out how the artist proceeded, what sized brushes he used, and how his

65
William Dyce
Christ as the Man of Sorrows
1860

66
William Bell Scott
Una and the Lion
1860

67
William McTaggart
The Storm
1890

68
Sir James Guthrie
A Hind's Daughter
1883

hand moved across the canvas – even indeed what the surface is made of. It is almost as if these were regarded as indecent secrets to be covered up and ignored. 'Finish' meant disguising the attributes of the hand-made object. A moral significance was attached to the notion of finishing a picture. To the purchaser an 'unfinished' picture gave the same poor value for money as an unvarnished mahogany table still scarred by the marks of plane and chisel.

The respect for finish was not a uniquely Scottish characteristic. Indeed it seems to have been universal in western art, and it is against the background of this deep respect for finish as the hallmark of quality and guarantee of value, that one needs to view developments in Scottish art which took place in the 1880s and 1890s. Whatever the differences between McTaggart's *Storm* and Guthrie's *Hind's Daughter* – to take examples from Edinburgh and Glasgow – they have one major feature in common. Both are clearly made by hand, using oil paint applied with the brush, or occasionally the knife, onto a canvas surface. No amount of realism of subject matter, nor acuity of perception, nor carrying of canvases into back gardens, or onto windy beaches to observe truthful light effects, counteracts the anti-naturalist disclaimer, as it were inscribed across the pictures – their determined insistence that the spectator look at paint as paint and see the hand-painting process in the making as an important feature in the final result. This reaction against machine-like finish was one point of agreement between the 'foreign' Glasgow School painting and the 'native' tradition followed by the pupils of Robert Scott Lauder.

The work of Lauder's most prominent pupils, George Paul Chalmers and William McTaggart, who stayed in Scotland, and John Pettie and William Quiller Orchardson, who moved to London, represents the last flowering of the

Wilkie, William Allan and Lauder school of Scottish art. Continental influences in the form of Hague School paintings can be seen at work on Chalmers and McTaggart, and various French influences can be detected in Orchardson. Nevertheless the work of all four remains quite distinct and apart from the kind of Continental art which was to strike Britain in the 1880s, and which can be seen in the English Newlyn or Scottish Glasgow School pictures.

Chalmers was essentially a painter of interior, McTaggart of exterior spaces. In both men the motive of personal artistic integrity was paramount, and their working careers represent continuing searches or quests, tragically cut short in Chalmers' case by his early death. Chalmers was a tonal painter, looking for beauty in the atmospheric mesh of interwoven colours out of which the deceptively grey shadows and half tones of dimly lit rooms are made. McTaggart, on the other hand, was a painter of the open air, of huge expanding spaces, cornfields, hills, beaches and seas. His method of painting these on site and his increasingly light and brilliant palette have led observers to claim him as one either influenced by French Impressionism, or as the discoverer of his own, uniquely Scottish brand of Impressionism. In truth McTaggart's aims were very different from those of the Impressionists. There was a depth of feeling in his response to the landscapes he knew best which is reminiscent of Constable. His paintings seem the outcome of a desire to understand the relation of human beings to the natural environment and to see the world with the unexploitive clarity of a child. It is rare that either his land or seascapes are unpeopled and the occupants are usually children.

In *The Storm*, his most famous painting, a small fishing community is shown contending with the elements in an effort to rescue a boat in danger of running onto the rocks. The force and fury of the sea are recurrent motifs in Scottish art from Runciman's *Lear*, through Thomson of Duddingston's *Fast Castle* and on to such twentieth century artists as Joan Eardley.

Of those Lauder pupils who moved to London, Orchardson was the last and

69
George Paul Chalmers
John Hutchison, Sculptor

MCTAGGART

70 *(left below)*
George Paul Chalmers
The Legend
1864–78

71 *(right below)*
William McTaggart
Spring
1864

72 Sir William Quiller Orchardson
    The Rivals
    1895
73 John Pettie
    William Quiller Orchardson
74 Sir William Quiller Orchardson
    The Queen of the Swords (study)
    *c.*1877

also the most refined and subtle of the narrative painters in the tradition of Wilkie. Seeking his subjects at times in· recorded moments of eighteenth and nineteenth century European history, at others in ostensibly trivial passages in fashionable drawing room life of the 1790s or 1890s, he balanced penetrating psychological insight with a highly sensitive eye for the abstract qualities of line, space and colour. He was a master of the daring use of nearly empty spaces, and

of a restricted range of pastel colours, amongst which sudden sharp touches of
pink or blue sing out like a high note. At the period, in the 1890s, when 'literary'
or narrative painting was being regarded with increasing disfavour by advanced
critics, Orchardson could lull such critics into the belief that his ironic behav-
ioural comedies were no more than aesthetic arrangements in colour harmony.
His work was admired in France – he received a gold medal in Paris in 1889 and
in 1895 was created *Chevalier de l'ordre de la légion d'honneur* – but no-one would
ever mistake it for the product of a man who had studied under the French sys-
tem or who practised French techniques.

The initial Glasgow School style was of hybrid, mainly of continental origin.
This had spread like lightening, at the end of the 1870s, and during the early
1880s, across most of Western Europe and Britain, and had even touched the
U.S.A. It entailed an astonishing degree of uniformity in the range of colours
employed, the application of pigment, and even in the subject matter chosen for
representation. In its ubiquitousness and its standardisation it resembled the
international Gothic style which had spread and flourished all over Europe
many centuries earlier. Taking paintings such as MacGregor's *Vegetable Stall* or
Guthrie's *Hind's Daughter* as exemplars of Glasgow School style prior to the mid

75
Sir James Lawton Wingate
A Summer's Evening
1888

1880s, one notes certain common features. These are the use of opaque and heavily applied pigment, which still retains the record of palette knife or hog's bristle, indicating that it was planted in firm blocks and left, unsmoothed, where it landed. These blocked conjunctions of colour and tone give each surface they are intended to describe – whether this is a turnip, a cabbage or a child's skirt and hands – a set of abrupt transitions, so that the forms appear faceted, as if carved out of wood. In its highly sophisticated crudeness such a style suggests peasant art adopted by painters who are themselves far from peasanthood.

The subject matter which went with this style was generally rural, of the farmyard, cottage and field, the going out and returning to labour, treated in a way that was deliberately anti-picturesque. Similar subjects, handled in a different style, can be seen in Edinburgh artists' work of the same period. Despite the insistence of such Glasgow pictures upon the monotonous and harsh conditions of rural existence, they do not convince one that such insistence was at all central to the artists' own intentions, and one is probably wrong in looking amongst these pictures for any social message. The studio talk of the day – as far at least as it can be gathered from private letters and reviews in journals such as *Scottish Art Review* – was purely formalist. Style rather than subject occupied these artists' thoughts – and they disliked story-telling or sentimental subjects. The advanced Scottish painter of the early 1890s might be expected to have worked – if only for a short time – in a Parisian or Belgian atelier, or to have close contacts with those who had done so. The word *valeurs* (tonal values) would drop readily from

76
William York MacGregor
Vegetable Stall
1884

76A
Detail

77
James Paterson
Autumn in Glencairn, Moniaive
1887

79
John Phillip
La Gloria
1864

his lips, and the name of Velázquez, the master of tonal values, would be uttered with deepest respect

There had already been an early foretaste of this interest in the paintings of John Phillip, who commenced as a rural Scottish genre painter in the manner of Wilkie but who, after three visits to Spain, abandoned his Scottish subject matter, his translucent brown shadows and his stage-like pictorial arrangements in favour of positive tonal contrasts, opaque pigment, a range of sharp pinks, reds, lemons and blacks, and a compositional format which turned the picture into an extension of the viewer's space. He clung, nevertheless, to narrative themes, and *La Gloria*, his masterpiece, is a hybrid picture. Superficially it is a study of whirling movement, blazing sunlight and dense shadow, which examined at leisure turns out to relate a story through facial expression, gesture and response, in the traditional way established by Wilkie.

Such hybridisation of traditional Scottish subjects with a continental style can also be seen at a later date in the work of John Henry Lorimer, especially perhaps in his *Ordination of Elders*. The larger and less finished of Wilkie's two paintings of *Knox dispensing the Sacrament* would have been familiar to Lorimer from his student days, since it had been purchased by the R.S.A. at Wilkie's sale of 1842, and Wilkie's picture provides the native stock upon which Lorimer's foreign compositional type was grafted. Lorimer's French training under Carolus Duran appears in his tonal treatment, and in the way in which the forms of these elderly, rugged faces, and of the bulky shoulders under the badly fitting coats are blocked out in broad planes. Duran had taught him to admire Velázquez, and Lorimer's extensive use of black may be one by-product of this admiration. The forceful expressions and characters of the Elders' patently rural heads, are, too,

PHILLIP

LORIMER

78
Sir John Lavery
The Dutch Cocoa House at the Glasgow International Exhibition of 1888
1888

very reminiscent of the early Velázquez peasant subject variously called *The Topers* or *The Worship of Bacchus*. Lorimer, following the newest Continental practises, treated his canvas as an extension of the spectator's own space, thrusting the viewer – who must be occupying a front pew – up against the edge of the table.

In some ways such hybridisations between native and foreign methods produced paintings of greater intrinsic interest than those of the almost wholly international Glasgow School. This school soon lost any homogeneity of style it had possessed. A number of the artists turned to portraiture and abandoned the square brushstroke of the 1880s for more fluent and bravura styles reminiscent of Whistler and Sargent. Others, like Hornel and Henry, moved away from naturalism towards increasingly decorative and abstracted colouristic and textural effects, encouraged by the popularity in Scotland of the work of the French artist Monticelli, and by the new interest in Japanese art and design.

HORNEL

CAMERON

Amongst the more interesting artists operating in Glasgow and Edinburgh at the end of the century were two, D. Y. Cameron and John Duncan, whose main careers lie in the present century. As an etcher, Cameron was predisposed

to emphasize tonal qualities in his painting. Indeed his oil paintings show a peculiar combination of line with areas of massed and deep shadow, which he must
surely have learnt whilst biting and printing his copper plates. His landscapes
bear much the same resemblance to real ones as an art school cast of the flayed
figure of an athlete bears to a living body. They are flayed landscapes – stripped
of softening cover, pared away to muscle and essential bone. They have an ex-
traordinary austerity and often exude a sense of being uninhabited and uninhab-
itable. Unlike McTaggart, or the generality of the Glasgow School artists,
Cameron did not reject mountainous view painting. He drew exactly the same
kind of scenery that McCulloch might have done before him, but rejected
McCulloch's glamour and over lush emotion, preserving instead an almost in-
human detachment that – in a work such as *The Hill of the Winds* – suggests
something very primitive, elemental and uncanny. As a much travelled artist,
and an exhibitor with the London International Society of Painters, Sculptors
and Engravers, Cameron would have been well acquainted with many facets of
modern Continental art. What is interesting about Cameron's work, however,
is the degree to which it preserves, underneath the new visual apparatus im-

82
Edward Atkinson Hornel
Kite Flying, Japan   *c.*1894

ported from the Continent, concerns which were part of an innately Scottish tradition, and which might have been recognised and partially approved by Thomson of Duddingston. *The Hill of the Winds* belongs, if it belongs anywhere, with the painting of the Celtic Revival, rather than with that of the Glasgow School.

DUNCAN

Cameron's austere Celticism is, however, a far cry from John Duncan's *St Bride*, with its evocation of an imaginary Celtic world of mythical Christianity. Duncan's work is highly eclectic, with stylistic derivations from later Pre-Raphaelitism, from Continental Symbolism, from early Renaissance fresco and from Celtic illuminated manuscripts. It offers a strange mixture of the naturalistic and the decorative, and a range of light and brilliant colours not unlike the later palette of the 'Scottish Colourists' in the 1920s. Those Scottish art-historians who have favoured painterly naturalism have tended to regard Duncan's work as freakish and isolated, but its connections with other British and Continental movements can be demonstrated, and there are also links with the earlier fantastic paintings of Noel Paton.

It is appropriate, perhaps, to conclude this essay with the work of a man who also became Director of the National Galleries of Scotland, and an historian of Scottish art. Stanley Cursiter's *Twilight* is a large painting, an intimate group of the artist's family and friends as if seen by another friend within the circle. Lamplight provides a very subdued glow on the faces and dresses within the room. Beyond the tall sash window the lights of Queen Street and of more distant blocks of Edinburgh buildings twinkle. It is possible to look at this painting as if it were an aggregate of many artists' works. In the background is a Whistler *Nocturne*; in the middle plane are portrait heads in the later styles of the Glasgow School artists George Henry, Alexander Roche, or E. A. Walton; in the foreground coffee pot, cups and roses group into a still-life painted by the young Peploe in his early manner. To see the picture like this is not to deny its innate consistency of lighting and compositional cohesiveness, nor to imply that Cursiter would have done far better to have painted three smaller pictures instead of one large one, but to recognise that his *Twilight* is a resumé of certain tendencies that had dominated Scottish art for the last twenty years – tendencies that were now, on the eve of war, due for extinction.

84
Stanley Cursiter
Twilight
1914

III
The Twentieth Century

Patrick Elliott

It cannot be said that twentieth-century painting in Scotland expresses a particular Scottish ethos, or that there is even a readily definable Scottish school. Although certain characteristics recur in modern Scottish painting, and are perhaps peculiar to it, Scottish art is none the less very much part of a wider, international current. The vibrant colours and lively brushwork of the French Impressionists, Post-Impressionists and Fauves profoundly influenced the development of Scottish twentieth-century art and American abstract painting too has marked much of the painting of the 1960s and 1970s. It is notoriously difficult even to agree on who can be counted a Scottish artist, since many have left Scotland at an early age and owe nothing to what could loosely be termed a 'Scottish tradition'. Duncan Grant and William Scott are just two of the painters who fall into this category. Conversely there are artists like Joan Eardley, who, though born in England, have studied at Art Schools in Scotland and have spent their entire careers north of the border.

It has often been said that bright colour and 'painterly' brushwork are particular characteristics of twentieth-century Scottish art. Perhaps more telling is the favour Scottish artists have shown for painting landscapes and still lifes which in some senses can be interpreted as archetypally Scottish themes, reflections of pride in the countryside and a liking for modest, utilitarian objects (Scottish still lifes tend to feature ordinary cups, teapots and flowers, rather than lavish table-top displays). The nude, so popular in Continental art, has never been a popular subject for Scottish artists, no doubt on account of the strong Calvinist ethic and partly also because of the climate. Similarly, narrative painting and complex subject matter have not been much favoured this century, nor has abstraction, nor has art with a strongly theoretical base. Instead Scottish artists have tended to depict objects and phenomena which can be seen with the eye and have employed a style which could broadly be termed 'naturalistic'.

Like many twentieth-century Scottish artists, James Pryde studied in Paris, where in the late 1880s he trained under the fashionable painter William Bouguereau. From 1890 he lived in London, collaborating with his brother-in-

85
William Gear
Marine Finistère No.2 August 1950
(detail)

86
James Pryde
Lumber: A Silhouette
1921

law William Nicholson under the name of the 'Beggerstaff Brothers', and earning a high reputation for his poster designs. Stylistically Pryde's pictures are close to those of Nicholson and of a sombre tonal range but the subjects he chose are steeped in memories of his native Edinburgh. *Lumber: A Silhouette* belongs to a series of thirteen works – begun in about 1909 and still in progress at Pryde's death – which were inspired by Mary, Queen of Scots's four-poster bed at Holyrood House. These haunting paintings have a strong theatrical element, reflecting Pryde's interest in the stage (in the 1890s he had even tried his hand at acting and later he designed theatre sets), and also evoke a peculiarly melancholic, unworldly atmosphere.

Living in London, Pryde exercised little influence on Scottish painting, and the same can be said of John Quinton Pringle, though for rather different reasons. Pringle was born in Glasgow and lived there all his life, but he rarely exhibited and was by profession an optician; he only began painting full-time three years before his death. He took evening courses at Glasgow School of Art and was very much influenced by the late nineteenth-century work of Bastien Lepage and the Hague School which had so impressed the Glasgow Boys. In works such as *Poultry Yard, Gartcosh*, Pringle employed their technique of dabbing paint on to the canvas in small, neat marks, a method which also has a rapport with that of Seurat and the neo-Impressionists.

Although best known as an architect and designer, Charles Rennie Mackintosh was also a watercolourist of great originality. His closely-observed studies of plants have a remarkable freshness and simplicity but they were rarely exhibited and only became widely known after his death. Although a number of Glasgow artists adopted his *art nouveau* style of draughtsmanship at the turn of the century, Mackintosh's work had a greater long-term impact on Viennese art

87
John Quinton Pringle
Poultry Yard, Gartcosh
1906

THE COLOURISTS

than it did on Scottish art. Apparently disillusioned by the lack of recognition at home, he left Scotland in 1914 and eventually settled in the South of France.

Mackintosh, Pryde and Pringle were all highly individual talents whose work had little effect on the development of Scottish art. The same cannot be said of the 'Colourists' who exerted such a profound impact on Scottish painting that even today their influence can be detected. The four painters known collectively as the 'Scottish Colourists' (and by custom, always identified by their initials rather than by their christian names) were S.J. Peploe, J.D. Fergusson, G. L. Hunter and F.C.B. Cadell. The four were not unified by any shared enterprise or creed and cannot be classified as a 'School'; indeed the group term 'Scottish Colourists' seems to have been first employed on the occasion of an exhibition held in 1948 when three of the four were already dead. Although Peploe and

Fergusson were very close, Hunter was aloof from the others and Cadell hardly knew Fergusson. What they did have in common though was their love of brilliant colour, acquired largely through their knowledge of the works of French painters such as Cézanne, Gauguin and Matisse. All except Hunter studied in Paris at formative stages in their careers and all four were to spend lengthy periods painting in France.

Each of the four Colourists exhibited regularly with the Glasgow-based dealer Alexander Reid who in 1923 organised a group show of Hunter, Cadell and Peploe at the Leicester Galleries in London. The following year, Reid arranged a further show in Paris, and added works by Fergusson; this was the first exhibition to feature all four artists. The same group showed together in 1925, again at the Leicester Galleries. These exhibitions gave the impression that the four formed a distinct Scottish school and subsequent exhibitions and catalogues have consolidated this notion. What has become obscured is that the four had quite different aims and methods.

Peploe and Fergusson were both born in Edinburgh and came from comfortable middle-class backgrounds. Peploe spent several months studying in Paris in 1894 (under Bouguereau, Pryde's teacher) and Fergusson did likewise in about 1895. They met shortly after 1900 and thereafter became the closest of friends, often spending vacations painting together. Fergusson later described their relationship as 'one of the best friendships that has ever been between two painters'. Struck by the painting of Manet and the Impressionists, both spent much time in France, Fergusson spending virtually every summer there from the mid 1890s onwards before moving there permanently in 1907. From about 1904 Peploe regularly spent his summers in France, joining Fergusson on painting holidays on the coast, and settling in Paris from 1910–12.

The early works of Peploe and Fergusson owe much to Manet and Frans Hals in the restricted palette of dark and light tones employed and also in the deft, painterly technique. Peploe was particularly gifted in this method of painting and in *The Green Blouse*, a portrait of the flower girl Jeannie Blyth, animates the figure with quick, lively brush-strokes. Fergusson too was attracted in the early years of the century to tonal painting, as evidenced in his *Self-portrait*, but from around 1906 both he and Peploe fell under the influence of Matisse and the Fauves and began to lighten their palettes and paint with pure, vibrant colour. Fergusson produced some of his finest works in his portraiture of 1905–10, a period in which he moved easily in the Bohemian Parisian café society and encountered many of the leading figures of the French *avant-garde*. Anne Estelle Rice was an American painter resident in Paris and was for a while one of Fergusson's closest friends. In his 1908 portrait of her, Fergusson has used brilliant colour, boldly outlined, to create an image of startling presence and verve quite distinct from the tonal portraits he had been making a few years earlier.

89
S. J. Peploe
The Green Blouse
c.1905

90
J. D. Fergusson
Anne Estelle Rice
1908

91
Stanley Cursiter
The Regatta
1913

Fergusson produced a number of portraits and figure compositions in the years around 1910–20 but during the same period, Peploe turned increasingly to still lifes and landscape and thereafter painted few portraits. From about 1910, both artists adopted Cézanne's technique of using short, tightly grouped brush-strokes and to an extent, both also experimented with aspects of the newly emerging style of Cubism. Although neither took the principle fully on board, both began to tighten up their compositions and replace the loose, painterly ef-fects with a more developed sense of geometric structure. Peploe and Fergusson were not the only Scottish artists to embrace aspects of European *avant-garde* painting. In 1913, Stanley Curstier produced a remarkable series of seven paint-ings much indebted to Italian Futurism, examples of which he had probably seen in London the previous year. Cursiter produced his own variants, amongst which was *The Regatta*. As in all Cursiter's Futurist works, forms are never frag-mented beyond recognition and the picture's impact derives more from the geometry of the sails themselves than from any radical compositional treatment Cursiter has brought to it; his painting is comfortably modern rather than aggressively *avant-garde*. Following his brief flirtation with Futurism, Cursiter reverted to painting accomplished but unadventurous works.

Born in Leith, near Edinburgh, F. C. B. Cadell was some ten years younger than Peploe and Fergusson. He took up painting at an early age and from 1899–1902 studied in Paris. He had his first exhibition in 1909 at the Edinburgh Gallery of Aitken Dott, the same year as Peploe's one-man show there. When

CADELL

92
F.C.B. Cadell
Still Life (The Grey Fan)

93
G. L. Hunter
Reflections, Balloch
1929–30

Peploe returned from France to Edinburgh in 1912, the two became close friends and the older artist's technique exerted a strong influence on Cadell's work of the period. After the war, Peploe's and Cadell's work developed in a similar direction: both turned increasingly to bright, primary colours applied flatly with little tonal modulation. But whereas Peploe concentrated almost exclusively on still lifes, Cadell favoured painting interiors to which he gave a deep sense of perspective. Even in his still lifes, such as *Still Life (The Grey Fan)*, the perspectival angle is very acute, while at the same time a strong sense of geometry is retained.

HUNTER

Although George Leslie Hunter is always linked with Peploe, Fergusson and Cadell as one of the four Colourists, in retrospect he seems to be the odd man out. He had a highly strung temperament and although he knew the other three, was rather distant from them. He was based in Glasgow, while Peploe and Cadell preferred Edinburgh and Fergusson France, and while the others had some degree of formal art training, and had all studied in at art schools in Paris, Hunter was entirely self-taught and only spent extended periods in France towards the end of his life. Born at Rothesay, on the Isle of Bute, Hunter moved with his family to San Francisco in 1892 when only thirteen years old and suffered the great misfortune of having many works destroyed in the 1906 earthquake on the eve of a solo exhibition. He returned to Scotland the following year and was soon taken up by the Glasgow dealer Alexander Reid who gave him his first exhibition in 1913. Peploe, Fergusson and Cadell shared a quest for tight geometric design and clarity of colour, but Hunter's brushwork is far more agitated and sometimes lacks control. There is often a sense of struggle in his works, contrasting with the great technical dexterity of the other three. But although his feeling for overall design was never as strong as theirs, his best pictures, such as *Reflections, Balloch*, achieve a great sense of freshness and unforced spontaneity.

The Colourists had looked to France for inspiration and the same was true of the generation of artists who reached maturity in the 1920s. William Gillies, John Maxwell, William Crozier, Anne Redpath and William Johnstone all spent extended periods in France and all were deeply affected by the experience. Art students studying in Scotland were fortunate in having a wide range of travelling scholarships available which permitted prolonged study abroad. But artists did not necessarily have to leave Scotland to see contemporary European painting. The Royal Scottish Academy in Edinburgh and the Royal Glasgow Institute regularly exhibited works by the leading Continental artists of the day, and indeed, many international artists showed in Scotland before they showed elsewhere in Britain. Works by Derain, Matisse, Picasso, de Segonzac and others could be seen during the 1920s and special exhibitions at the Royal Scottish Academy included those of Edvard Munch in 1931 and Paul Klee in 1934.

William Gillies was born in Haddington, East Lothian, attended Edinburgh

94
Sir William Gillies
Flowers on a Sideboard

College of Art, and in 1924 won a scholarship to study in Paris with the Cubist painter André Lhote. Lhote, who was then at the height of his fame, taught a number of Scottish artists and was much admired by the then principal at Edinburgh College of Art, Morley Fletcher. However, his dry form of Cubism failed to impress Gillies. By the early 1930s Gillies was looking more to the Expressionist style of the Norwiegan painter Edvard Munch, but throughout the 1930s borrowed styles with imaginative eclecticism, reflecting interest in the art of Bonnard, Klee, Matisse and Braque. A debt to Matisse is evident in *Flowers on a Sideboard*, in which energetic rhythms are created across the whole canvas through the repetition of curving forms. What remained stable in Gillies' art was his subject matter: still lifes and landscapes, principally of the Lothian, Fife and Border regions. Although not as well known outside Scotland as the Colourists, Gillies' influence and legacy was perhaps as marked as theirs, due to his teaching at Edinburgh College of Art where he remained from 1926 until his retirement as principal in 1966.

Another teacher at the College of Art in Edinburgh was John Maxwell, a close friend of Gillies and his colleague at the College from 1929 to 1943 and again in the 1950s. Maxwell studied in Paris at the Académie Moderne with Fernand Léger and Amadée Ozenfant around 1927, but like Gillies he abandoned experiments with Cubism early on and opted instead for a more conventional technique. He and Gillies regularly went on painting holidays together

95
John Maxwell
View from a Tent
1933

and it was on the occasion of one of these trips that Maxwell painted *View From a Tent*. The scene is of the sands of Morar on the West Coast, glimpsed from the tent which the two artists shared. Subsequently, Maxwell's work became increasingly 'primitive' in character. Perspective is flattened and detail rendered with a child-like directness and simplicity which at times recalls the art of Klee and Chagall whose work he much admired.

    The same type of primitivising is found in the painting of Anne Redpath. Born at Galashiels in the Borders, she studied at Edinburgh College of Art and

96
Anne Redpath
The Mantlepiece
1944

REDPATH

then, following her marriage in 1920, moved to France where she raised a family and virtually abandoned painting. She returned to Scotland in 1934 at the age of thirty-nine and began again to devote time to her art. Like Gillies, she was particularly attracted to the work of Matisse. In *The Mantlepiece* of 1944, perspective has been 'tipped-up' to give a flattened, richly decorative effect, and colour and form have been skilfully choreographed across the entire surface to make the room come to life. Redpath had a great fondness for ordinary, domestic objects such as cups and teapots and these recur in many of her still lifes. In her later work, she took to using richly coloured paint which was applied with a palette knife and built up into a thick, jewel-like impasto.

CROZIER

William Crozier was born in Edinburgh and after attending Edinburgh College of Art, won a scholarship to Paris where he studied under André Lhote. Unlike Gillies and Maxwell, who managed to shrug off the Cubist methods they had learned in Paris, Crozier was more strongly marked. In *Edinburgh (from Salisbury Crags)* Crozier articulates the cubic structure of each building with great clarity, rather than simply giving an impression of spatial recession; the brushwork is also very square and regular. Crozier died young but the works he did complete suggest a talent quite distinct from his fellow Edinburgh-trained artists, reflecting a search for geometric clarity rather than loose, painterly effects.

MACTAGGART

In his short career, Crozier gained a significant reputation among his fellow artists, among whom William MacTaggart, grandson of the painter William McTaggart. MacTaggart trained at Edinburgh College of Art and subsequently

97
William Crozier
Edinburgh (from Salisbury Crags)
1927

shared studios with Crozier and Gillies. Ill health prevented him from prolonged study in Paris but in the 1920s he regularly went on painting holidays in France and in 1924 held his first one-man show at the Scottish Church in Cannes in the South of France. Like Gillies, he absorbed influences from Continental art in a very creative fashion, drawing from Derain, de Segonzac and Munch in particular. From his earliest works, MacTaggart applied paint thickly and vigorously, and during the 1950s began laying paint on in a dense, richly-coloured impasto to acheive an effect close to stained-glass, such as in *Poppies Against the Night Sky*.

Although, as we have seen, a good number of Scottish artists were in touch with 'advanced' art movements on the Continent during the 1920s, there was a marked reluctance to assimilate *avant-garde* tendencies. In general, Scottish artists and collectors were attracted to a domesticated modernism of bright colour and gentle distortion rather than to the more threatening forms proposed by Picasso and the Surrealists. It was perhaps on account of this dearth of interest in a radically modern art that William Johnstone and William McCance chose to live for much of their lives outside Scotland, even though they passionately loved their native land.

The son of a farmer, William Johnstone attended Edinburgh College of Art from 1919–23 and then in 1925 went to Paris on a Carnegie travelling scholarship. He studied, like so many other Scots, with the Cubist painter André Lhote, but also fell under the influence of the Surrealists. He returned to Scotland in 1927, settling briefly in Selkirk where he painted *Painting, Selkirk,*

98
William MacTaggart
Poppies against the Night Sky

JOHNSTONE

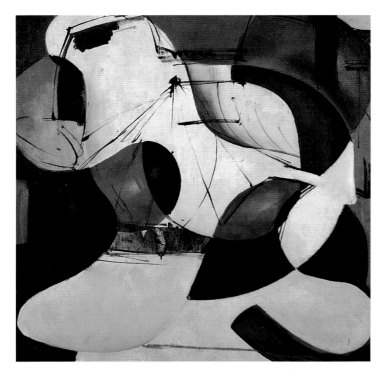

99
William Johnstone
Painting, Selkirk,
Summer 1927

COWIE

Summer 1927. It was altered at a later date (Johnstone re-worked many of his paintings which makes dating them difficult) when slight adjustments to the abstract forms were made and the calligraphic black lines added. The title was also given some years later. Failing to find success in Scotland, Johnstone and his American wife moved to California in 1928, but returned the following year and eventually settled in London in 1931. There he pursued a successful teaching career, becoming principal of Camberwell School of Art & Crafts from 1938–46 and from 1947–60 principal at the Central School, and also writing influential studies on modern art and primitivism. Never one to conform, Johnstone retired to the Borders and became a sheep farmer and in his last years produced a quantity of large and highly innovative abstract works.

William McCance's career has evident parallels with Johnstone's. McCance was born at Cambuslang near Glasgow and attended Glasgow School of Art. He moved to London in 1920 and shortly afterwards produced what are probably the first abstract oil-paintings made by a Scottish artist, works which certainly owe something to Wyndham Lewis and the Vorticists in the way objects are treated almost as machine components, but which also convey a sense of organic growth. McCance made his living as an illustrator and art critic, making regular contributions to a variety of magazines including *The Spectator*. Joseph Brewer, whose portrait McCance painted in 1925, was an American writer working for the same magazine. McCance was passionately fond of books and many of his portraits feature the sitter reading. From 1930–33 he was controller of the famous Gregynog private press in Wales which produced high quality limited edition books, and in the 1940s and 1950s lectured in typography and book production at Reading University. Like Johnstone he moved back to Scotland on his retirement.

It has often been argued that students from Edinburgh College of Art showed a tendency to adopt a rich, painterly technique, while those at Glasgow School of Art showed a preference for linear qualities and the figure. James Cowie, a Glasgow-trained artist, certainly embodied these latter qualities. Born in Cuminestown, Aberdeenshire, Cowie studied at Glasgow School of Art and subsequently became art master at Bellshill Academy and then from 1937–48 warden of Hospitalfield House, a post-graduate summer schoool for art near Arbroath. He frequently used his pupils as models, for example in *Portrait Group* begun in 1932 and substantially reworked in about 1940. The female figure in the foreground, originally portrayed as a young girl, was then changed into a mature woman, and the other figures were subtly altered. Drapery was added at the top, a hedge in the middle ground and the table cloth changed from a striped design to one with patterned squares (strangely, Cowie repainted the stripes in the portion on the right). Cowie's works often have a peculiarly wooden, unnatural feel, largely due to the fact that he evolved compositions in a piecemeal

fashion, joining together individual studies rather than considering the painting as a whole. The rendering of spatial depth is ambiguous, for example in the way the chair in the foreground relates to the table. At times, this stiffness was unintentional, but at others it was a quality deliberately adopted. In his late work in particular, Cowie strove to make his compositions as enigmatic as possible, making novel experiments with perspective and scale and clearly borrowing from the surrealism of Paul Nash.

William Oliphant Hutchison was director at Glasgow School of Art from 1933–43 and evolved a painting style quite similar to Cowie's though his ambitions were limited largely to conventional portraiture. Born in Kirkcaldy, he studied at Edinburgh College of Art and in 1920 moved to London where he became friendly with James Pryde. The *Portrait of A Home Guardsman* is a fine example of Hutchison's work, combining close observation and great sensitivity.

102   William Oliphant Hutchison
Portrait of a Home Guardsman 1940

Two of the most original British artists of the 1940s and 1950s trained at Glasgow School of Art during Hutchison's directorship and from 1937–38 studied under Cowie at Hospitalfield: Robert Colquhoun and Robert MacBryde. Known as 'The Two Roberts', they met at the School of Art and were thereafter inseparable; when Colquhoun won a travelling scholarship, extra money had to be found for MacBryde for they insisted on going together. They even collaborated together on some works. Both moved to London in 1941 where they

shared a studio with the Neo-Romantic painter John Minton and encountered
Jankel Adler, a Polish artist who had developed a hybrid form of Cubism in the
1930s. Much influenced by him, the two Roberts adopted a Cubist-inspired
style of twisted, tortured forms framed within angular contours. Colquhoun is
usually considered the more inventive of the two, but at his best, MacBryde
could produce work of great power. *Still Life* of *c.*1947 is a highly accomplished
work, redolent of the lean post-war years in its sparseness and almost mono-

103
Robert MacBryde
Still Life
*c.*1947

· 89 ·

chromatic gloom. Where the Colourists might have chosen flowers and gaily coloured crockery, MacBryde went instead for objects with unusual, often aggressive shapes. Alongside Picasso and de Chirico, MacBryde was able to make his still lifes look slightly intimidating, a sensation derived in this case from the strange combination of a water-melon and a backgammon set and the contrast between the round forms of one and the angular forms of the other. The two looming shadows add a further disturbing note. It is difficult not to associate the tension in such works with the famously tempestuous relationship between the two Roberts. Both drank heavily and both died comparatively young. Colquhoun's work displays a ferocity similar to that of MacBryde's, but is often on a grander scale, for example in the large *Figures in a Farmyard* of 1953. The sense of post-war anguish evoked in such canvases has its nearest British rival in the art of Francis Bacon, who knew the two Roberts well.

104   Robert Colquhoun
Figures in a Farmyard 1953

105
Alan Davie
Seascape Erotic
1955

DAVIE & GEAR

MacBryde and Colquhoun were inspired by Cubism, and as such, were looking to a style of painting which had a history dating back some forty years. Alan Davie and William Gear were inspired by – or one should say, helped create – a style of painting which only emerged in the 1940s. Davie was born in Grangemouth on the Firth of Forth and studied at Edinburgh College of Art under John Maxwell. In 1947 he won a scholarship from the College which enabled him to travel on the continent and see contemporary American abstract expressionist painting by Jackson Pollock and Mark Rothko (amongst others) in Peggy Guggenheim's collection in Venice. Excited by their free, gestural method of applying paint, and by the large scale of their works, Davie adopted a comparable technique. In *Seascape Erotic*, forms are loosely suggested but not precisely defined; the emphasis is rather on the rhythm and tremendous energy of the paint itself. Commenting on the work, Davie wrote that it expressed 'no premeditated intention or idea', rather the forms and colours were arrived at spontaneously. An analogy between Davie's painting and improvised music is pertinent since he worked for a time as a professional jazz musician.

William Gear turned not to American painting for inspiration, but to contemporary European art, becoming a member of the CoBrA movement which emerged in the late 1940s (the initials stand for Copenhagen, Brussels and Amsterdam, cities from which many members of the group came). Gear travelled widely during and after the war before settling in Paris from 1947–50 (as did his fellow Scots the sculptors Eduardo Paolozzi and William Turnbull). In Paris Gear produced a series of vibrantly coloured paintings, such as *Marine Finistère No.2 August 1950*, which although apparently abstract, are often derived from landscape motifs.

Since 1950, Gear has lived in England. One of the most remarkable artists to move in the opposite direction, from England to Scotland, was Joan Eardley. Born in Sussex, Eardley moved to Glasgow in 1939 and enrolled at the School of Art the following year. She studied briefly under Cowie at Hospitalfield and from 1948–49 spent a productive time in Italy on a travelling scholarship. Perhaps because she was an outsider, Eardley was immediately impressed by aspects of life which now seem demonstrably Scottish but which other Scottish-born

106
William Gear
Marine Finistère No.2 August 1950

E A R D L E Y

107
Joan Eardley
Catterline in Winter
c.1963

108
John Bellany
Kinlochbervie
1966

artists had chosen to ignore. Her studies of children in the depressed Gorbals area of Glasgow are remarkably observed, as are her landscapes and seascapes executed at the small coastal village of Catterline, such as *Catterline in Winter.* The houses seem as if they are huddling together, bracing themselves for a long, hard winter. Eardley's works have the freedom of execution one finds in abstract painting but also carry the emotional weight abstraction sometimes lacks: they are full of lived experience, conveying a reaction to the landscape which is at once fresh and powerful.

BELLANY

The same could be said of John Bellany's work. He too has drawn on aspects of Scotland's sea-faring culture and he too has taken his art close but never fully into abstraction. Born in 1942 in the fishing village of Port Seton near Edinburgh, his father and both grandfathers were fishermen. Although he chose to become an artist, training at Edinburgh College of Art, fishing imagery has dominated his painting with tenacious atavism. *Kinlochbervie* is an early work, executed when the artist was still a student at the Royal College of Art in London. Even at this stage, Bellany was developing the rich and complex symbolism which would remain the hallmark of his art. Themes of the Last Supper, the Crucifixion and death (in the gutting of the fish) are woven into his personal experience of village fishing life.

It has already been mentioned that Glasgow artists have shown a particular tendency towards hard-edged realism and Cowie was noted in this respect. Glasgow-born Mark Boyle has taken this obsession with realism to its limit. Boyle studied law and did not attend art college, but by the early 1960s was becoming interested in performance art. In 1964, he and his companion Joan Hills began duplicating randomly-chosen sections of earth, a practice they have since continued with the help of their two children under the name of 'Boyle Family'. In making a work such as *Study for the Broken Path Series with Border Edging*, a portion of earth is coated with a rubber-like gel, a fibreglass cast of this is made and then painted to achieve what is effectively an exact replica. Boyle has remarked that 'the aim is to produce as objective a work as possible', free from 'originality, style and significance'. But of course, all art is significant in one sense or another, and the Boyles' work is very much of its epoch in expressing the idea that anything can be art, that art is all around us, that the apparently ordinary can be fascinating if examined closely.

Boyle and Hills moved to London in the early 1960s as did John Bellany and the performance artist Bruce McLean. This is a move a great many Scottish artists have made this century. For a long time it was felt that making a successful

109
Boyle Family
Study for the Broken Path Series with Border Edging
1986

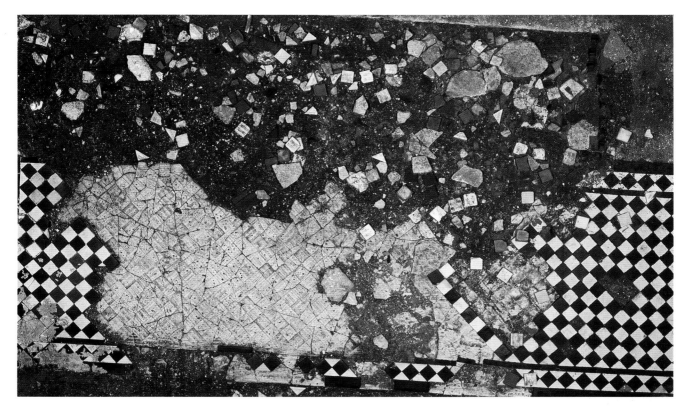

career as an artist and leaving Scotland were two sides of the same coin. London's attraction as a centre of the art market has traditionally pulled artists into its orbit, but this pattern is beginning to change. Artists like Robin Philipson, Jack Knox and Sandy Moffat have, through their teaching at Edinburgh, Dundee and Glasgow respectively, fostered a greater sense of confidence among young artists. Moffat, a close friend of John Bellany from the early 1960s, has been a guiding inspiration to students at Glasgow School of Art during the 1980s. His portraits, such as that of the poet Norman MacCaig, have often been of writers and artists with strong Scottish connections, affirming the belief in an independent, national culture.

Ken Currie studied under Moffat at Glasgow School of Art and originally intended becoming a film maker, but disillusioned with the problems in financing films turned instead to painting. His deeply held Socialist convictions have found expression in such works as *The Glasgow Triptych*. The three panels, each nearly three metres across, relate separate moments in twentieth-century working class history in Glasgow. *Young Glasgow Communists*, the third part of the triptych, is a manifesto-like composition, grouping together the various tools and influences which have shaped Currie's art. The artist himself is seated at the right in a blue cap. A Fernand Léger poster is unrolled beside him, a book on the Mexican mural painter Diego Rivera is seen in his bag along with paint brushes, a camera is strapped over his back and a book by the Italian Marxist writer Gramsci is visible under the seated woman.

NEW GLASGOW BOYS

Other Glasgow-trained figurative painters, notably Steven Campbell, Peter Howson, Stephen Conroy and Adrian Wiszniewski have attracted much critical attention and a success which has earned them the title of the 'New Glasgow Boys', after their late nineteenth-century counterparts. What is more, they have all elected to remain in Scotland – a sign which bodes well for the future of Scottish art.

111
Ken Currie
Young Glasgow Communists
(from *Glasgow Triptych*)
1986

111A
Detail

Index of Artists and Illustrations

SNGMA 3034

ALAN DAVIE
born 1920

105 *Seascape Erotic* 1955
oil on board 160 × 241
SNGMA 1084

SIR WILLIAM FETTES
DOUGLAS
1822 − 1891

62 *The Spell* 1864
oil on canvas 77.5 × 157
NGS 779

JAMES DRUMMOND
1816 − 1877

61 *The Porteous Mob* 1855
oil on canvas 112 × 143
NGS 180

JOHN DUNCAN
1866 − 1945

83 *St Bride* 1913
tempera on canvas 120.7 × 143.5
NGS 2043

THOMAS DUNCAN
1807 − 1845

55 *Portrait of 'Christopher North'
(Professor John Wilson)*
oil on millboard 60.6 × 42.5
SNPG 1369

WILLIAM DYCE
1806 − 1864

65 *Christ as the Man of Sorrows* 1860
oil on millboard 34.9 × 48.4

NGS 2410

JOAN EARDLEY
1921 − 1963

107 *Catterline in Winter* c. 1963
oil on board 120.7 × 130.8
SNGMA 888

J. D. FERGUSSON
1874 − 1961

88 *Self-portrait* c. 1902
oil on canvas 50.8 × 56.4
SNPG 2515

90 *Anne Estelle Rice* 1908
oil on board 66.5 × 57.5
SNGMA 1247

WILLIAM GEAR
born 1915

85 *Marine Finistère No. 2 August 1950*
& 1950
106 oil on canvas 65.4 × 54.6
SNGMA 3299

ANDREW GEDDES
1783 − 1844

39 *Portrait of David Wilkie* 1816
oil on panel 66 × 48.2
SNPG 1443

WALTER GEIKIE
1795 − 1837

46 *Scottish Roadside Scene*
oil on canvas 40.6 × 61
NGS 1825

SIR WILLIAM GILLIES
1898 − 1973

94 *Flowers on a Sideboard*
oil on canvas 88 × 124

SNGMA 1759

SIR JOHN WATSON
GORDON
1788 − 1864

34 *James Hogg ('The Ettrick Shepherd')* 1830
oil on canvas 127 × 101.6
SNPG 2718

SIR JAMES GUTHRIE
1859 − 1930

68 *A Hind's Daughter* 1883
oil on canvas 91.5 × 76.2
NGS 2142

GAVIN HAMILTON
1723 − 1798

36 *Andromache Bewailing the Death of Hector*
oil on canvas 64.2 × 98.5
NGS 2428

GAWEN HAMILTON
about 1697 − 1737

12 *Nicol Graham of Gartmore and Two
Friends, Seated in a Library*
oil on canvas 63.5 × 60.5
NGS 2464

SIR GEORGE HARVEY
1806 − 1876

47 *The Curlers* (study) c. 1835
oil on canvas 35.9 × 79.4
NGS 1579

EDWARD ATKINSON
HORNEL
1864 − 1933

82 *Kite Flying, Japan* c. 1894
oil on canvas 76 × 48

NGS 1815

G. L. HUNTER
1879 – 1931

93 *Reflections, Balloch* 1929 – 30
oil on canvas 63.5 × 76.2
SNGMA 18

WILLIAM OLIPHANT HUTCHISON
1889 – 1970

102 *Portrait of a Home Guardsman* 1940
oil on canvas 76 × 55.6
SNPG 2719

GEORGE JAMESONE
1589/90 – 1644

2 *Mary Erskine, Countess Marischal*
1626
oil on canvas 67.3 × 54.6
NGS 958

WILLIAM JOHNSTONE
1897 – 1981

99 *Painting, Selkirk, Summer 1927*
1927 – 38, 1951
oil on canvas 101.6 × 101.6
SNGMA 1100

ROBERT SCOTT LAUDER
1803 – 1869

56 *Christ Teacheth Humility* 1847
oil on canvas 234 × 353
NGS 221

58 *Portrait of David Roberts in Oriental
Dress* 1840
oil on canvas 133 × 101.5

SNPG 2466

SIR JOHN LAVERY
1865 – 1941

78 *The Dutch Cocoa House at the
Glasgow International Exhibition of
1888* 1888
oil on canvas 45.8 × 35.7
NGS 2431

WILLIAM HOME LIZARS
1788 – 1859

45 *Reading the Will* 1811
oil on panel 51.5 × 64.8
NGS 423

JOHN HENRY LORIMER
1856 – 1936

80 *Ordination of Elders* 1891
oil on canvas 109.2 × 140
NGS 1879

ROBERT MacBRYDE
1913 – 1966

103 *Still Life c.* 1947
oil on canvas 41.5 × 87
SNGMA 3497

WILLIAM McCANCE
1894 – 1970

100 *Portrait of Joseph Brewer* 1925
oil on canvas 71 × 61
SNGMA 3446

HORATIO McCULLOCH
1805 – 1867

60 *Inverlochy Castle* 1857
oil on canvas 90.2 × 151
NGS 288

WILLIAM YORK MacGREGOR
1855 – 1923

76 *Vegetable Stall* 1884
oil on canvas 105.5 × 150.5
NGS 1915

WILLIAM McTAGGART
1835 – 1910

67 *The Storm* 1890
oil on canvas 121.9 × 183
NGS 1834

71 *Spring* 1864
oil on canvas 45.1 × 60.4
NGS 2137

WILLIAM MacTAGGART
1903 – 1981

98 *Poppies against the Night Sky c.* 1962
oil on board 76.2 × 63.5
SNGMA 1046

DAVID MARTIN
1737 – 1797

24 *Professor James Russell with his Son
James* 1769
oil on canvas 101.6 × 127.7
SNPG 2014

JOHN MAXWELL
1905 – 1962

95 *View from a Tent* 1933
oil on canvas 76.2 × 91.5
SNGMA 977

ALEXANDER MOFFAT
born 1943

110 *Portrait of Norman MacCaig* 1968
oil on canvas 121.8 × 91.4
SNPG 2231

JACOB MORE
1740 – 1793

48 *The Falls of Clyde (Cora Linn)*
oil on canvas 79.4 × 100.4
NGS 1897

ALEXANDER NASMYTH
1758 – 1840

30 *Robert Burns*
oil on panel 61.1 × 44.5
SNPG 1062

35 *The Building of the Royal*
& *Institution* 1825
49 oil on canvas 122.5 × 165.5
(Anonymous Loan to the NGS)

50 *Edinburgh Castle and the Nor' Loch* 1824
oil on canvas 45 × 60.3
NGS 2104

JAMES NORIE
1684 – 1757

10 *Classical Landscape with Architecture* 1736
oil on canvas 64.8 × 132
NGS 1768

SIR WILLIAM QUILLER
ORCHARDSON
1832 – 1910

72 *The Rivals* 1895
oil on canvas 84 × 117
NGS 2184

74 *The Queen of the Swords* (study)
c. 1877
oil on canvas 47.3 × 80.6
NGS 1018

JAMES PATERSON
1854 – 1932

77 *Autumn in Glencairn, Moniaive* 1887
oil on canvas 102 × 127
NGS 2424

SIR JOSEPH NOEL
PATON
1821 – 1901

63 *The Quarrel of Oberon and Titania* 1849
oil on canvas 99 × 152
NGS 293

64 *Dawn: Luther at Erfurt* 1861
oil on canvas 92.7 × 69
NGS 1230

S. J. PEPLOE
1871 – 1935

89 *The Green Blouse c.* 1905
oil on wood 50.8 × 50.2
SNGMA 28

JOHN PETTIE
1839 – 1893

73 *Portrait of William Quiller Orchardson*
oil on canvas 40.6 × 35.5
SNPG 875

JOHN PHILLIP
1817 – 1867

79 *La Gloria* 1864
oil on canvas 144 × 217
NGS 836

JOHN QUINTON
PRINGLE
1864 – 1925

87 *Poultry Yard, Gartcosh* 1906
oil on canvas 62.3 × 75.6
SNGMA 37

JAMES PRYDE
1866 – 1941

86 *Lumber: A Silhouette* 1921
oil on canvas 182.9 × 152.4
SNGMA 1521

SIR HENRY RAEBURN
1756 – 1823

25 *James Hutton*
oil on canvas 125.1 × 104.8
SNPG 2686

26 *Lieutenant-Colonel Lyon* 1788
oil on canvas 90.2 × 68.6
NGS 1224

27 *The Reverend Robert Walker skating*
on Duddingston Loch
oil on canvas 76.2 × 63.5
NGS 2112

28 *David Hunter of Blackness*
oil on canvas 76 × 61.5
NGS 2394

31 *Colonel Alastair Macdonell of Glengarry*
oil on canvas 241 × 150
NGS 420

32 *Mrs Scott Moncrieff*
oil on canvas 75 × 62.3
NGS 302

33 *Self-portrait*
oil on canvas 89.5 × 69.9
NGS 930

ALLAN RAMSAY
1713 – 1784

17 *The Painter's Wife (Anne Bayne)*
    oil on canvas 68.3 × 54.7
    SNPG 2603

18 *Sir Peter Halkett Wedderburn* 1746
    oil on canvas 74.3 × 61.6
    NGS 1960

19 *Hew Dalrymple, Lord Drummore* 1754
    oil on canvas 127 × 102.2
    SNPG 2800

20 *The Painter's Wife (Margaret Lindsay)*
    oil on canvas 76.2 × 63.5
    NGS 430

22 *Mrs Bruce of Arnot*
    oil on canvas 73.7 × 61
    NGS 946

21 *David Hume* 1766
    oil on canvas 76.2 × 63.5
    SNPG 1057

23 *Jean-Jacques Rousseau* 1766
    oil on canvas 75 × 64.8
    NGS 820

ANNE REDPATH
1895 – 1965

96 *The Mantlepiece* 1944
    oil on board 59.5 × 59.5
    SNGMA 1960

DAVID ROBERTS
1796 – 1864

59 *Rome – Sunset from the Convent of
    San Onofrio on Mount Janiculum* 1856
    oil on canvas 213 × 427
    NGS 304

ALEXANDER RUNCIMAN
1736 – 1785

15 *Self-portrait with John Brown* 1784
    oil on canvas 63.6 × 76.5
    SNPGL 31 (On loan from the National
    Museums of Scotland)

JOHN RUNCIMAN
1744 – 1768

14 *Self-portrait* 1767
    oil on canvas 68.7 × 55.6
    SNPGL 32 (On loan from the National
    Museums of Scotland)

38 *King Lear* 1767
    oil on panel 44.8 × 61
    NGS 570

DAVID SCOTT
1806 – 1849

52 *The Traitor's Gate* 1842
    oil on panel 137 × 183.4
    NGS 843

WILLIAM BELL SCOTT
1811 – 1890

66 *Una and the Lion* 1860
    oil on canvas 91.5 × 71
    NGS 2367

JOHN THOMAS SETON
flourished 1759 – 1806

13 *William Fullerton of Carstairs and
    Ninian Lowis* 1773
    oil on canvas 74.3 × 61.6
    NGS 1837

ARCHIBALD SKIRVING
1749 – 1819

29 *Mrs John Wilson*
    pastel on paper 68.5 x 56
    SNPG 2613

THE REV JOHN
THOMSON
1778 – 1840

51 *Fast Castle from Below*
    (possibly 1824)
    oil on canvas 76.2 × 105.4
    NGS 2039

ADRIAN VAN SON
flourished 1581 – 1602

1   *James VI and I* 1595
    oil on panel 72.9 × 59.9
    SNPG 156

RICHARD WAITT
died 1732

6   *Self-portrait* 1728
    oil on canvas 60.7 × 127
    SNPG 2142

7   *Kenneth Sutherland, 3rd Lord Duffus*
    oil on canvas 203.2 × 140.6
    SNPG 1095

THOMAS WARRENDER
flourished 1673 – 1713

8   *Still-life*
    oil on canvas 59.1 × 74.3
    NGS 2404

SIR DAVID WILKIE
1785 – 1841

41 *Portrait of William (Chalmers) Bethune,*
    his Wife Isobel Morison and their
    Daughter Isabella 1804
    oil on canvas 125.7 × 102.9
    NGS 2433

42 *Pitlessie Fair* 1804
    oil on canvas 58.5 × 106.7
    NGS 1527

43 *The Letter of Introduction* 1813
    oil on panel 61 × 50.2
    NGS 1890

44 *John Knox Dispensing the Sacrament*
    at Calder House (study) *c.* 1837 – 40
    oil on panel 45.1 x 61
    NGS 2172

57 *The Irish Whiskey Still* 1840
    oil on panel 119.4 × 158
    NGS 2130

SIR JAMES LAWTON
WINGATE
1846 – 1924

75 *A Summer's Evening* 1888
    oil on canvas 54.5 × 74.3
    NGS 1649

JOHN MICHAEL
WRIGHT
1617 – 1694

4   *Lord Mungo Murray*
    oil on canvas 224.8 × 154.3
    SNPG 997

5   *Sir William Bruce* 1664
    oil on canvas 72.4 × 61
    SNPG 894

Select Bibliography

I: GENERAL HISTORIES (IN ORDER OF PUBLICATION)

Robert Brydal
Art in Scotland, Edinburgh 1889

David Martin
The Glasgow School of Painting
London 1902

William Darling McKay
The Scottish School of Painting
London 1906

Sir James Caw
Scottish Painting Past and Present
London 1908

J. D. Fergusson
Modern Scottish Painting
Glasgow 1943

William MacLellan
The New Scottish Group
Glasgow 1947

Stanley Cursiter
Scottish Art, London 1949

T. J. Honeyman
*Three Scottish Colourists, Peploe, Cadell,
Hunter*, Edinburgh 1950

M. R. Apted
The Painted Ceilings of Scotland 1550–1650
Edinburgh 1966

T. J. Honeyman, William Hardie,
Ailsa Tanner
Three Scottish Colourists
Exhibition catalogue
Scottish Arts Council, Edinburgh 1970

Duncan Thomson
Painting in Scotland 1570 – 1650
Exhibition catalogue
Scottish National Portrait Gallery 1975

David and Francina Irwin
Scottish Painters at Home and Abroad
London 1975

Esme Gordon
The Royal Scottish Academy 1826 – 1976
Edinburgh 1976

William Hardie
Scottish Painting 1837 – 1939
London 1976

Edward Gage
*The Eye in the Wind: Contemporary
Scottish Painting Since 1945*
London 1977

Cordelia Oliver
Painters in Parallel
Exhibition catalogue
Edinburgh College of Art 1978

Lindsay Errington
*Master Class: Robert Scott Lauder and
his Pupils*
Exhibition catalogue
National Gallery of Scotland 1983

Roger Billcliffe
The Glasgow Boys, London 1985

Alexander Moffat
New Image Glasgow
Exhibition catalogue
Third Eye Centre Glasgow 1985

Duncan Macmillan
Painting in Scotland: The Golden Age
Oxford 1986

The Vigorous Imagination
Exhibition catalogue
Scottish National Gallery of Modern Art
1987

James Holloway
*Patrons and Painters: Art in Scotland
1650 – 1760*
Exhibition catalogue
Scottish National Portrait Gallery 1989

Keith Hartley
Scottish Art Since 1900
Exhibition catalogue
Lund Humphries in association with the
Scottish National Gallery of Modern Art
1989

Roger Billcliffe
The Scottish Colourists, London 1989

Duncan Macmillan
Scottish Art 1460 – 1990
(to be published Edinburgh 1990)

Paul Harris
*Dictionary of Scottish Painters
1600 – 1960*
(to be published Edinburgh 1990)

II: INDIVIDUAL ARTISTS (IN ALPHABETICAL ORDER)

AIKMAN
James Holloway, *William Aikman*
Scottish Masters Series
National Galleries of Scotland 1988

ALLAN
T. Crouther Gordon
David Allan the Scottish Hogarth
privately published Scotland 1951

CARSE
Lindsay Errington, *Alexander Carse*
Scottish Masters Series
National Galleries of Scotland 1987

CHALMERS
Edward Pinnington
*George Paul Chalmers RSA and the Art of
His Time*, Glasgow 1896

DYCE
Marcia Pointon, *William Dyce*
Oxford 1979

EARDLEY
Fiona Pearson, *Joan Eardley*
Scottish Masters Series
National Galleries of Scotland 1988

VAN DER GOES
*Hugo van der Goes and the Trinity Panels
in Edinburgh*
National Gallery of Scotland 1974

GUTHRIE
Sir James L. Caw, *Sir James Guthrie*
London 1932

HERDMAN
Lindsay Errington, *Robert Herdman*
Scottish Masters Series
National Galleries of Scotland 1988

JAMESONE
Duncan Thomson
The Life and Art of George Jamesone
Oxford 1974

LAVERY
Kenneth McConkey, *Sir John Lavery*
Ulster Museum, Belfast and the Fine Art
Society, London 1984

MCCULLOCH
Sheena Smith, *Horatio McCulloch*
Glasgow Museums and Art Galleries
1988

MCTAGGART
Lindsay Errington
William McTaggart 1835-1910
Exhibition catalogue, National Gallery
of Scotland 1989

MEDINA
Rosalind Marshall, *John de Medina*
Scottish Masters Series,
National Galleries of Scotland 1988

MORE
James Holloway, *Jacob More*
Scottish Masters Series
National Galleries of Scotland 1987

ORCHARDSON
Hilda Orchardson Gray
The Life of William Quiller Orchardson
London 1930

PETTIE
Martin Hardie, *John Pettie*
London 1908

RAEBURN
Sir Walter Armstrong, *Sir Henry Raeburn*
London 1901

Raeburn Bi-Centenary Exhibition
Exhibition catalogue
National Gallery of Scotland 1956

RAMSAY
Alastair Smart
The Life and Art of Allan Ramsay
London 1952

Allan Ramsay, his Masters and Rivals
Exhibition catalogue
National Gallery of Scotland 1963

ROBERTS
Helen Guiterman and Briony Llewellyn
David Roberts
Phaidon Press and the Barbican Art
Gallery, London 1986

SCOTT
William Bell Scott,
Memoir of David Scott RSA
Edinburgh 1850

Mungo Campbell, *David Scott*
Scottish Masters Series
National Galleries of Scotland 1990

THOMSON
William Baird
John Thomson of Duddingston
Edinburgh 1895

WILKIE
Allan Cunningham
The Life of Sir David Wilkie
3 vols, London 1843

Lindsay Errington, *A Tribute to Wilkie*
Exhibition catalogue
National Gallery of Scotland 1985

Lindsay Errington, *Sir David Wilkie*
Scottish Masters Series
National Galleries of Scotland 1988

WRIGHT
Sara Stevenson and Duncan Thomson
John Michael Wright: the King's Painter
Exhibition catalogue
Scottish National Portrait Gallery 1982